4th Workshop on Narrative Understanding (WNU2022)

Online
15 July 2022

ISBN: 978-1-7138-5645-0

Printed from e-media with permission by:

Curran Associates, Inc.
57 Morehouse Lane
Red Hook, NY 12571

Some format issues inherent in the e-media version may also appear in this print version.

Association for Computational Linguistics
209 N. Eighth Street
Stroudsburg, Pennsylvania 18360

Phone: 1-570-476-8006
Fax: 1-570-476-0860

acl@aclweb.org

Additional copies of this publication are available from:

Curran Associates, Inc.
57 Morehouse Lane
Red Hook, NY 12571 USA
Phone: 845-758-0400
Fax: 845-758-2633
Email: curran@proceedings.com
Web: www.proceedings.com

WNU 2022

The 4th Workshop of Narrative Understanding (WNU2022)

Proceedings of the Workshop

July 15, 2022

Order copies of this and other ACL proceedings from:

Association for Computational Linguistics (ACL)
209 N. Eighth Street
Stroudsburg, PA 18360
USA
Tel: +1-570-476-8006
Fax: +1-570-476-0860
acl@aclweb.org

Introduction

Welcome to the 4th Workshop on Narrative Understanding!
This is the 4th iteration of the workshop, which brings together an **interdisciplinary** group of researchers from AI, ML, NLP, Computer Vision and other related fields, as well as scholars from the humanities to discuss **methods to improve automatic narrative understanding capabilities.**
We are happy to present 8 papers on this topic (along with 7 non-archival papers to be presented only at the workshop). These papers take on the complex challenges presented by diverse texts in areas of film, dialogue and literature as they look to improve methods for event extraction, gender and representation bias, controllable generation, quality assessment, and other tasks related to the workshop theme. We would like to thank everyone who submitted their work to this workshop and the program committee for their helpful feedback.
We would also like to thank our invited speakers for their participation in this workshop: Maria Antoniak, Yejin Choi, Dan Goldwasser, and Andrew Piper.

Faeze, Elizabeth, Khyathi, Nader, Mohit, and Snigdha

Organizing Committee

Organizers

Nader Akoury, University of Massachusetts Amherst, USA
Faeze Brahman, Allen Institute for AI, USA
Khyathi Chandu, Meta AI, USA
Snigdha Chaturvedi, University of North Carolina, Chapel Hill, USA
Elizabeth Clark, Google Research, USA
Mohit Iyyer, University of Massachusetts Amherst, USA

Program Committee

Apoorv Agarwal, Text IQ
Antoine Bosselut, EPFL
David Bamman, UC Berkeley
Saadia Gabriel, University of Washington
Andrew Gordon, University of Southern California
Ari Holtzman, University of Washington
Yangfeng Ji, University of Virginia
Marzena Karpinska, University of Massachusetts Amherst
Roman Klinger, University of Stuttgart, Germany
Ashutosh Modi, Indian Institute of Technology, Kanpur, India
Shashank Srivastava, University of North Carolina, Chapel Hill
Shiv Surya, University of North Carolina, Chapel Hill
Katherine Thai, University of Massachusetts Amherst
Anvesh Rao Vijjini, University of North Carolina, Chapel Hill
Chao Zhao, University of North Carolina, Chapel Hill

Keynote Talk: The Abduction of Sherlock Holmes

Yejin Choi
University of Washington, AI2

Abstract: Understanding narrative requires abductive reasoning about the best explanations to partial observations, which in turn, requires commonsense knowledge about how the world works. In this talk, I will discuss recent advances on abductive reasoning and commonsense knowledge induction.

Bio: Yejin Choi is Brett Helsel professor at the Paul G. Allen School of Computer Science & Engineering at the University of Washington and also a senior research manager at AI2 overseeing the project Mosaic. Her research investigates a wide variety problems across NLP and AI including commonsense knowledge and reasoning, neural language (de-)generation, language grounding with vision and experience, and AI for social good. She is a co-recipient of the ACL Test of Time award in 2021, the CVPR Longuet-Higgins Prize (test of time award) in 2021, a NeurIPS Outstanding Paper Award in 2021, the AAAI Outstanding Paper Award in 2020, the Borg Early Career Award (BECA) in 2018, the inaugural Alexa Prize Challenge in 2017, IEEE AI's 10 to Watch in 2016, and the ICCV Marr Prize (best paper award) in 2013. She received her Ph.D. in Computer Science at Cornell University and BS in Computer Science and Engineering at Seoul National University in Korea.

Keynote Talk: Towards Interactive Neuro-Symbolic Narrative Analysis on Social Media

Dan Goldwasser
Purdue University

Abstract: Social media is the new town square, where influential ideas are raised and debated. Understanding the narratives in these public debates is an important yet highly challenging task, requiring models that can deal with narratives built collaboratively by multiple users, each contributing short and often noisy texts. For example, a statement such as "we demand the supreme court make the right decision" can only be understood as part of a broader discussion. In this talk, I will discuss some recent and on-going work that exploits the rich social context available on social media platforms to help narrative analysis and suggest an interactive framework for several different narrative analysis tasks, capturing the main themes of the narratives and attitudes towards entities mentioned in them.

Bio: Dan Goldwasser is an Associate Professor at the Department of Computer Science at Purdue University. He is broadly interested in connecting natural language with real world scenarios and using them to guide natural language understanding. His current interests focus on grounding political discourse to support understanding real-world scenarios, using neuro-symbolic representations. Dan Completed his PhD in Computer Science at the University of Illinois at Urbana-Champaign and was a postdoctoral researcher at the University of Maryland. He has received research support from the NSF, including a recent CAREER award, DARPA and Google.

Keynote Talk: The Shape of Stories: A Research Program

Andrew Piper
McGill University

Abstract: How we tell stories is a core aspect of any story's meaning. Whether it is a tale of epiphany (St. Augustine Confessions), decline (Gibbon's Decline and Fall of the Roman Empire), or salvation (The New Testament), human stories assume shapes that transcend the meaning of the individual events contained within them. Recent work in computational narrative understanding (or computational narratology) has developed a variety of approaches to measure the shape of stories, what we could more technically call "narrative form;" In this talk, I will showcase prominent recent examples – and challenges – for the computational modeling of narrative form. The goal of the talk is to outline a coherent theoretical and methodological framework for future work that aims at understanding the functions and effects of story shape in a variety of different social contexts.

Bio: Andrew Piper is Professor and William Dawson Scholar in the Department of Languages, Literatures and Cultures at McGill University in Canada. He is the editor of the *Journal of Cultural Analytics* and directs .txtlab, a laboratory for cultural analytics at McGill. He is the author of *Enumerations: Data and Literary Study* (Chicago 2018) and most recently, *Can We Be Wrong? The Problem of Textual Evidence in a Time of Data* (Cambridge 2020).

Keynote Talk: Storytelling in Online Communities

Maria Antoniak
Cornell University

Abstract: Where and why do people share stories online? How and why should we be interested in computationally modeling these stories? In this talk, we'll explore the different locations and motivations underlying the sharing of stories in online communities, as well as different approaches to computationally measuring and representing these stories. We'll contrast these data sources with other story datasets in natural language processing, discussing both the benefits and challenges of working with data drawn from internet forums, groups, and networks.

Bio: Maria Antoniak is a PhD candidate in Information Science at Cornell University and incoming Young Investigator at the Allen Institute for AI. Her research focuses on unsupervised natural language processing methods and applications to computational social science and cultural analytics. She has a master's degree in computational linguistics from the University of Washington, and she has completed research internships at Microsoft, Facebook, Twitter, and Pacific Northwest National Laboratory.

Table of Contents

Program

Friday, July 15, 2022

08:30 - 09:15	*Virtual Poster Session*
09:15 - 09:20	*Opening Remarks*
09:20 - 10:00	*Invited Talk 1*
10:00 - 10:30	*BREAK*
10:30 - 11:10	*Invited Talk 2*
11:10 - 11:50	*Invited Talk 3*
11:50 - 13:30	*LUNCH*
13:30 - 14:10	*Invited Talk 4*
14:10 - 15:00	*Panel Discussion*
15:00 - 15:30	*BREAK*
15:30 - 16:30	*Hybrid Poster Session*

Uncovering Surprising Event Boundaries in Narratives

Zhilin Wang, Anna Jafarpour, Maarten Sap
University of Washington
{zhilinw, annaja}@uw.edu, msap@cs.washington.edu

Abstract

When reading stories, people can naturally identify sentences in which a new event starts, i.e., *event boundaries*, using their knowledge of how events typically unfold, but a computational model to detect event boundaries is not yet available. We characterize and detect sentences with expected or surprising event boundaries in an annotated corpus of short diary-like stories, using a model that combines commonsense knowledge and narrative flow features with a RoBERTa classifier. Our results show that, while commonsense and narrative features can help improve performance overall, detecting event boundaries that are more subjective remains challenging for our model. We also find that sentences marking surprising event boundaries are less likely to be causally related to the preceding sentence, but are more likely to express emotional reactions of story characters, compared to sentences with no event boundary.

1 Introduction

When people read stories, they can easily detect the start of new events through changes in circumstances or in narrative development, i.e., *event boundaries* (Zacks et al., 2007; Bruni et al., 2014; Foster and Keane, 2015; Jafarpour et al., 2019b). These event boundaries can be expected or surprising. For example, in the story in Figure 1 based on crowdsourced annotation, "getting along with a dog who does not generally like new people" marks a *surprising* new event, while "their playing fetch together for a long time" is an *expected* new event.

We aim to study whether machines can detect these surprising or expected event boundaries, using commonsense knowledge and narrative flow features. Characterizing features that are informative in detecting event boundaries can help determine how humans apply expectations on event relationships (Schank and Abelson, 1977; Kurby and Zacks, 2009; Radvansky et al., 2014; Ünal

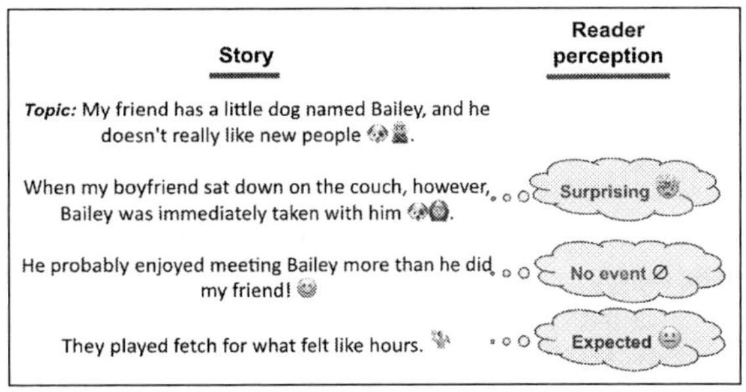

Figure 1: Example story with sentences that contain either a surprising event boundary, no event boundary or an expected event boundary respectively. The annotations of reader perception are from the Hippocorpus dataset (Sap et al., 2022).

et al., 2019; Zacks, 2020). Furthermore, detection of sentences with event boundaries can also be useful when generating engaging stories with a good amount of surprises. (Yao et al., 2019; Rashkin et al., 2020; Ghazarian et al., 2021).

To differentiate sentences with surprising event boundaries, expected event boundaries, and no event boundaries, we train a classifier using 3925 story sentences with human annotation of event boundaries from diary-like stories about people's everyday lives (Sap et al., 2022). We extract various commonsense and narrative features on relationships between sentences of a story, which can predict the type of event boundaries. Commonsense features include the likelihood that adjacent sentences are linked by commonsense relations from the knowledge graphs Atomic (Sap et al., 2019a) and Glucose (Mostafazadeh et al., 2020). Narrative features include Realis (Sims et al., 2019) that identifies the number of event-related words in a sentence, Sequentiality (Radford et al., 2019; Sap et al., 2022) based on the probability of generating a sentence with varying context and SimGen (Rosset, 2020), which measures the similarity between a sentence and the sentence that is most likely to

Proceedings of the 3rd Wordplay: When Language Meets Games Workshop (Wordplay 2022), pages 1 - 12
July 15, 2022 ©2022 Association for Computational Linguistics

be generated given the previous sentence. We then combine the prediction based on these features with the prediction from a RoBERTa classifier (Liu et al., 2019), to form overall predictions.

We evaluate the performance of the classification model by measuring F1 of the predictions and compare various configurations of the model to a baseline RoBERTa model. We find that integrating narrative and commonsense features with RoBERTa leads to a significant improvement (+2.2% F1) over a simple RoBERTa classifier. There are also individual differences on the subjective judgment of which sentences contain a surprising or an expected event boundary, that is reflected in the detection model's performance. The performance of our model increases with increasing agreement across the human annotators. Additionally, by interpreting the trained parameters of our model, we find that the absence of causal links between sentences is a strong predictor of surprising event boundaries.

To further analyze how surprising event boundaries relate to deviation from commonsense understanding, we compare the performance of the classification model on the related task of ROC Story Cloze Test (Mostafazadeh et al., 2016). This task concerns whether the ending sentence of a story follows/violates commonsense based on earlier sentences, which can be linked to whether sentences are expected or surprising. Our model performs significantly higher on the ROC Story Cloze Test (87.9% F1 vs 78.0% F1 on our task), showing that surprising event boundaries go beyond merely violating commonsense and therefore can be seen as more challenging to detect. Together, our results suggests that while detecting surprising event boundaries remains a challenging task for machines, a promising direction lies in utilizing commonsense knowledge and narrative features to augment language models.

2 Event Boundary Detection Task

Events have been widely studied in Natural Language Processing. They have often been represented in highly structured formats with word-specific triggers and arguments (Walker et al., 2006; Li et al., 2013; Chen et al., 2017; Sims et al., 2019; Mostafazadeh et al., 2020; Ahmad et al., 2021) or as Subject-Verb-Object-style (SVO) tuples extracted from syntactic parses (Chambers and Jurafsky, 2008; Martin et al., 2018; Rashkin et al., 2018; Sap et al., 2019a). In narratives, events are represented as a continuous flow with multiple boundaries marking new events (Zacks et al., 2007; Graesser et al., 1981; Kurby and Zacks, 2008; Zacks, 2020); however, we lack a model to detect the boundary events that mark the meaningful segmentation of a continuous story into discrete events.

In this work, we study stories from a cognitive angle to detect event boundaries. Such event boundaries relate to our narrative schema understanding (Schank and Abelson, 1977; Chambers and Jurafsky, 2008; Ryan, 2010), commonsense knowledge (Sap et al., 2019a; Mostafazadeh et al., 2020) and world knowledge (Nematzadeh et al., 2018; Bisk et al., 2020). Existing work has studied on salient (i.e. important/most report-able) event boundaries within a story (Ouyang and McKeown, 2015; Otake et al., 2020; Wilmot and Keller, 2021). However, missing from literature is how salient event boundary can either be surprising or expected based on the knowledge of how a flow of events should unfold. For example, events can be surprising when they deviate from commonsense in terms of what people would predict (e.g., if someone won something, they should not be sad; Sap et al., 2019a). Surprising events can also be low likelihood events (Foster and Keane, 2015) such as seeing someone wear shorts outside in winter, or due to a rapid shift in emotional valence between events (Wilson and Gilbert, 2008) such as seeing a protagonist being defeated. Importantly, there are individual differences in how humans segment narratives into events (Jafarpour et al., 2019a).

We tackle event boundary detection as a three-way classification task that involves distinguishing surprising but plausible event boundaries in story sentences from expected event boundaries and no event boundaries. To mirror how humans read stories, we predict the event boundary label for a sentence using all of its preceding sentences in the story, as well as the general story topic as context. *Surprising* event boundaries are novel events that are unexpected given their context, such as a dog getting along with someone despite not typically liking new people. *Expected* event boundaries are novel events that are not surprising, such as a person playing a new game with a dog for a long time given that they like each other. In contrast, sentences with *no event* boundary typically continue or elaborate on the preceding event, such as a person liking a dog given that they get along with the dog (Figure 1).

Majority label	#Samples (%)	% majority agreement (std)
No event	2255 (57.5)	68.1 (13.9)
Expected	650 (16.6)	58.8 (10.6)
Surprising	509 (13.0)	61.7 (11.9)
Tied	511 (13.0)	41.1 (5.7)
Total	3925 (100)	62.2 (15.2)

Table 1: Descriptive Statistics for Event-annotated sentences. Majority label refers to the most common annotation of a sample from 8 independent annotators. If there is a tie between 2 labels, it is categorized as tied. Majority agreement is the proportion of sample annotations for the majority label.

3 Event-annotated Data

We use the English-based Event-annotated sentences from stories in the Hippocorpus dataset to study event boundaries. This dataset contains 240 diary-like crowdsourced stories about everyday life experiences, each containing an average of 16.4 sentences and are annotated at the sentence level (Sap et al., 2022). Stories were inspected for the absence of offensive or person-identifying content. For the annotation, eight crowdworkers were shown a story sentence by sentence and were asked to mark whether each sentence contained a new surprising or expected event boundary, or no event boundary at all, based on their subjective judgment (Sap et al., 2022). Summarized in Table 1, based on the majoritarian vote, most sentences (57.5%) contain no event boundaries while 16.6% and 13.0% of sentences contains expected and surprising event boundaries, respectively.

Due to the inherent subjectivity of the task, aggregating labels into a majority label yields low agreement (e.g., 61.7% for surprising event boundaries; Table 1). Therefore, at training time, we use the proportion of annotations for each event boundary type as the label instead of the majority vote, because such distributional information is a better reflection of the inherent disagreement among human judgements (Pavlick and Kwiatkowski, 2019). At test time, we use the majority vote as a gold label, since measuring performance on distribution modelling is less intuitive to interpret, and subsequently break down performance by agreement level to take disagreements into account.

4 Event Boundary Detection Model

We first describe informative commonsense and narrative features that we extract for the event boundary detection model. Then, we describe how we integrate these features with a RoBERTa classifier in our model before detailing our experimental setup. Figure 2 depicts an overview of our model.

4.1 Features

We select a collection of commonsense features (Atomic and Glucose relations) and narrative flow features (Realis, Sequentiality and SimGen). A model is trained separately from our main model for Atomic relations, Glucose relations and Realis while models for Sequentiality and SimGen are used without further training. Features of story sentences are extracted as input into the main model. Because language modelling alone might not be sufficient to learn such features (Gordon and Van Durme, 2013; Sap et al., 2019a), we provide the extracted features to the model instead of relying on the language models to learn them implicitly.

Atomic relations are event relations from a social commonsense knowledge graph containing numerous events that can be related to one another (Sap et al., 2019a). The event relations in this graph consists of:

Emotional **React**ion,
The **Effect** of an event,
Want to do after the event,
What **Need**s to be done before an event,
The **Intent**ion to do a certain event,
What **Attr**ibutes an event expresses.

When an event affects the subject, the feature name is preceded by an `x`, while if it affects others, it has an `o`. `o` only applies to React, Effect and Want. For example, an `xWant` of a sentence *PersonX pays PersonY a compliment* is that *PersonX will want to chat with PersonY*, and an `oWant` is that *PersonY will compliment PersonX back*. We use Atomic relations because surprising event boundaries can involve breaches of commonsense understanding (Bosselut et al., 2019; Sap et al., 2019a; Mostafazadeh et al., 2020; Gabriel et al., 2021). Furthermore, some Atomic relations (`xReact` and `oReact`) concern emotional affect and therefore can be used to capture changes in emotional valence, which can cause events to be seen as surprising (Wilson and Gilbert, 2008).

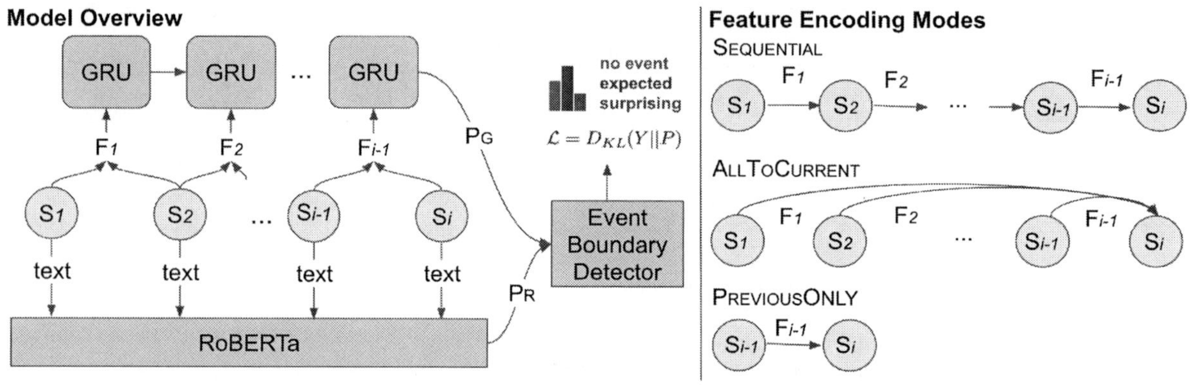

Figure 2: (Left) Our model involves a **GRU** to combine features from sentence pairs with three feature encoding modes, **RoBERTa** to consider story sentences and **Event Boundary Detector** to combine predictions made by the two components. S_n and F_n refer to sentence n and features n respectively, while P_G and P_R are predictions made by the GRU and RoBERTa. The output is a probability distribution over no event boundary, expected event boundary and surprising event boundary, which is used to update model parameters together with the label using the **Kullback-Leibler Divergence** loss function. (Right) **Features** (Atomic, Glucose, Realis, Sequentiality and SimGen) can be extracted as input into the GRU in three feature encoding modes: SEQUENTIAL (shown in Model Overview), ALLTOCURRENT and PREVIOUSONLY.

We train an Atomic relation classifier using a RoBERTa-base model (Liu et al., 2019) and the Atomic dataset to classify event-pairs into one of the nine possible relationship labels as well as a None label (to introduce negative samples). We achieved a validation F1 of 77.15%, which is high for a 10-way classification task. We describe training and other experimental details in the Appendix. When making inferences on the Event-annotated dataset, we predict the likelihood that a preceding sentence in a story will be related to the current sentence via each of the nine relationship labels. Because Atomic relations are directed relations (e.g., *I ate some cake* `xEffect` *I am full* is different from *I am full* `xEffect` *I ate some cake*), we also made the reverse inference in case commonsense relations between sentences exist in the reverse direction. Together, 9 forward atomic relation features and 9 reverse features (marked with'-r') are used.

Glucose relations are event relations from another commonsense knowledge dataset containing relations between event-pairs in 10 dimensions (Mostafazadeh et al., 2020). Glucose relation features are used to complement Atomic relation features in its coverage of commonsense relations. Dim-1 to 5 are described below while Dim-6 to 10 are the reverse/passive form of Dim-1 to 5 respectively.

`Dim-1`: **Event** that causes/enables
`Dim-2`: **Emotion**/human drive that motivates
`Dim-3`: **Change in location** that enables
`Dim-4`: **State of possession** that enables
`Dim-5`: **Other attribute** that enables

Glucose relation classifier was trained on a RoBERTa-base model to classify event-pairs from the Glucose dataset into one of ten possible relation labels as well as a None label. We used the *specific* version of Glucose events represented in natural language. As a result, we achieved a validation F1 of 80.94%. Training and other experimental details are in the Appendix. During inference on the Event-annotated dataset, we predict and use as features the likelihood that the current sentence will be related to a preceding sentence via each relation label.

Realis events are words that serve as triggers (i.e., head words) for structured event representations (Sims et al., 2019). Realis event words denote concrete events that actually happened, meaning that a higher number of Realis event words suggests greater likelihood of the sentence containing a new event boundary (expected or surprising). We trained a BERT-base model (Devlin et al., 2019) on an annotated corpus of literary novel extracts (Sims et al., 2019). We achieved a validation F1 of 81.85%, inspired by and on par with Sap et al. (2020). Then, we use the trained model to make inference on story sentences in the Event-annotated dataset. Finally, we used the number of `Realis` words in each sentence as a feature. Training and other experimental details are in the Appendix.

Sequentiality is a measure of the difference in conditional negative log-likelihood of generating a sentence given the previous sentence or otherwise (Sap et al., 2020, 2022). Sequentiality can be a predictor for unlikely events, which can cause surprise (Foster and Keane, 2015). We use GPT-2 (Radford et al., 2019) to measure this negative log-likelihood since it is a Left-to-Right model, which matches the order in which annotators were shown sentences in a story. NLL of each sentence was obtained in two different contexts. `NLL_topic` is based on the sentence alone with only the topic as prior context, while `NLL_topic+prev` uses the previous sentence as additional context to study the link between adjacent sentences. Finally, `Sequentiality` is obtained by taking their difference. Experimental details are in the Appendix.

$$NLL_{topic} = -\frac{1}{|s_i|} \log p_{LM}(s_i \mid Topic)$$

$$NLL_{topic+prev} = -\frac{1}{|s_i|} \log p_{LM}(s_i \mid Topic, s_{i-1})$$

SimGen is computed as the cosine similarity between each sentence and the most likely generated sentence given the previous sentence, under a large Left-to-Right language model (specifically, Turing-NLG; Rosset, 2020). Then, we separately converted the original sentence and generated sentence into sentence embeddings using a pre-trained MPnet-base model (Song et al., 2020). Finally, the generated embeddings and the original embeddings are compared for cosine similarity, which is used as a feature. Experimental details are in the Appendix.

4.2 Model Architecture

We propose a model to integrate feature-based prediction with language-based prediction of event boundaries, illustrated in Figure 2 (left). The predictions are independently made with extracted features using a gated recurrent unit (GRU) and with language (i.e., story sentences) using RoBERTa. Then these predictions are combined into a final predicted distribution for the three types of event boundaries. Our model is then trained using the Kullback-Leibler Divergence loss.

GRU is used to combine features relating the current sentence i to prior sentences in a story. It sequentially considers information concerning prior sentences, which mimics the annotator's procedure of identifying event boundaries as they read one sentence at the time. As seen in Figure 2 (right), we use three feature encoding modes to determine the features that are used as input into the GRU, as inspired by literature on event segmentation (Pettijohn and Radvansky, 2016; Baldassano et al., 2018; Zacks, 2020). These three modes represent different ways of facilitating information flow between sentences, which can have distinct effects on identifying event boundaries.

The first mode, SEQUENTIAL, encodes features from all previous sentences in the story in a recurrent way (1 to 2, 2 to 3 ... $i-1$ to i) up until the current sentence i. The second mode, ALLTOCURRENT, uses features from each of the previous sentences to the current sentence i (1 to i, 2 to i ... $i-1$ to i). The third mode, PREVIOUSONLY, ($i-1$ to i) only feeds into the GRU the features relating to the previous sentence. For all modes, the dimension of each time step input is K_G, representing the total number of distinct features. We then project the final output of the GRU, $h_G \in \mathbb{R}^{K_G}$, into a 3-dimensional vector space representing the unnormalized probability distribution over event boundary types.

RoBERTa is used to make predictions based on text in story sentences. We use all story sentences up to sentence i inclusive. We then project the hidden state of the first token (also known as CLS token), $h_R \in \mathbb{R}^{K_R}$, into a 3-dimensional space representing the unnormalized probability distribution over event boundary types.

Combining predictions We combine predictions made by the GRU (P_G) and RoBERTa (P_R) by concatenating their predictions and multiplying it with a linear classifier of size (6, 3) to output logits of size (3). The logits are then normalized using Softmax to give a distribution of the three types of event boundaries (P). The weights of the linear classifier are initialized by concatenating two identity matrix of size 3 ($\mathbf{I}_3$), which serves to perform elementwise addition between the predictions of the GRU and RoBERTa at early stages of the training process.

$$W := [\mathbf{I}_3; \mathbf{I}_3] \tag{1}$$

$$P := Softmax(W([P_G; P_R])) \tag{2}$$

Loss function We use the Kullback-Leibler Divergence loss function to train the model. We use it over the standard Cross Entropy loss function because our training targets are in the form: proportion of annotations for each type of event boundary (e.g., 0.75, 0.125, 0.125 for no event, expected and surprising respectively). Including such distributional information in our training targets over using the majority annotation only can reflect the inherent disagreement among human judgements (Pavlick and Kwiatkowski, 2019), which is important to capture for event boundaries given that they are subjective judgements.

4.3 Experimental setup

We seek to predict the event-boundary annotation for each Hippocorpus story sentence, using preceding sentences in the story as context, as shown in Figure 2. Additional training and experimental details are available in the Appendix.

K-fold Cross-validation Because of the limited size of the dataset (n=3925), we split the dataset in k-folds (k=10), using one fold (n=392) for validation and nine other folds combined for training. From each of the 10 models, we obtained the prediction for the validation set. Together, the validation sets for the 10 models combine to form predictions for the entire dataset, which we use to conduct significance testing in order to compare the performance of models.

GRU was accessed from PyTorch, with K_G set to 33 and a hidden dimension of 33.

RoBERTa RoBERTa-base-uncased with 12-layer, 768-hidden (K_R), 12-heads, 110M parameters, 0.1 dropout was used, accessed from HuggingFace Transformers library (Wolf et al., 2020). When more than 10 prior sentences are available in a story, we use only the most recent 10 sentences due to RoBERTa input sequence length limitations.

Evaluation Metrics While capturing distributional information of subjective judgement labels (Pavlick and Kwiatkowski, 2019) is important for training, it can also be difficult to interpret for evaluation. Therefore, we decided to predict for the most likely label during evaluation and compare it against the majority label for each sample. Some 511 (13.0%) samples do not have a single majority label (e.g., equal number of expected and surprising annotations) and these samples were excluded. We use micro-averaged F1 as the metric.

	overall F1	no event F1	expected F1	surprising F1
Event Detector (w RoBERTa)				
PREVIOUSONLY*	78.0	87.2	60.0	59.7
SEQUENTIAL	77.3	86.6	57.5	60.5
ALLTOCURRENT	76.9	86.3	57.5	59.7
RoBERTa	75.8	86.2	55.8	54.3
Event Detector (w/o RoBERTa)				
ALLTOCURRENT	63.9	81.8	32.3	24.8
SEQUENTIAL	63.8	82.1	34.6	19.5
PREVIOUSONLY	63.4	81.8	31.8	21.2

Table 2: Event detection task: Performance of Event Detector compared to baseline model. *: overall F1 significant different from RoBERTa based on McNemar's test ($p < 0.05$) (McNemar, 1947)

5 Results and Discussion

We first quantify the performance of our model in detecting event boundaries, using a coarse-grained performance measure on F1 with respect to majority vote. Then, we investigate how the performance varies based on annotation subjectivity. Finally, we inspect the model parameters to identify commonsense and narrative features that are most informative in detecting event boundaries.

Improving prediction of event boundaries As seen in Table 2, RoBERTa alone performs fairly well in predicting event boundaries (F1 = 75.8%, within 2.2% F1 of our best performing model), but can be further supported by our commonsense and narrative features to improve its performance. In contrast, the commonsense and narrative features alone do not perform as well.[1] Overall, our best performing set-up is the Event Detector (PREVIOUSONLY) with F1 = 78.0%, which is significantly different from RoBERTa alone based on McNemar's test ($p < 0.05$). [2] Its overall strong performance is largely contributed by its strong performance in detecting no event boundaries and expected event boundaries. F1 for no event boundary is higher than both surprising and expected event boundaries, likely because there are more sentences with no event boundaries as seen in Table 1. The PREVIOUSONLY configuration performs best for

[1]We also increased learning rate to 1e-3 for better performance given the absence of RoBERTa predictions in this ablation set-up.

[2]McNemar's test is used to determine whether samples that have been predicted accurately (or not) by one model overlap with those that have predicted accurately (or not) by another model.

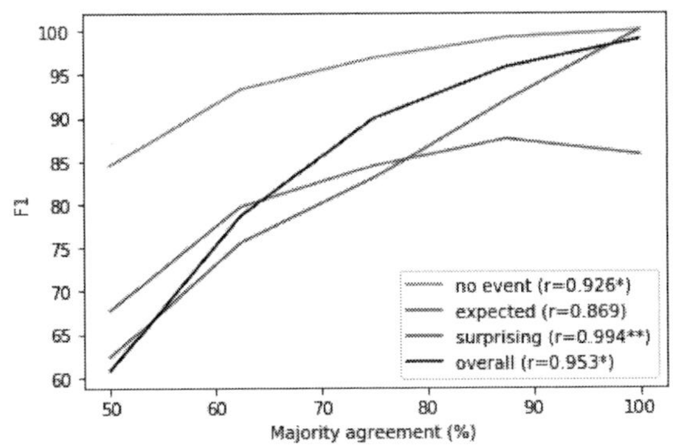

Figure 3: F1 by Event Detector (PREVIOUSONLY) against majority agreement, on all 10 folds. * means that Pearson's r is significant at $p < 0.05$ and ** at $p < 0.001$.

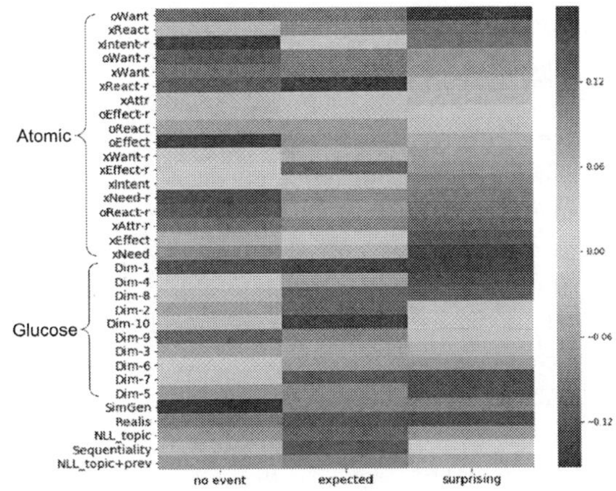

Figure 4: Feature weights towards each label in GRU component of Event Detector (PREVIOUSONLY)

no event boundaries and expected event boundaries likely because determining whether the current sentence continues an expected event (or not) requires retaining the latest information in working memory (Jafarpour et al., 2019a). However, the SEQUENTIAL configuration seems to perform the best in predicting surprising event boundaries. Compared to no/expected event boundaries, we hypothesize that predicting surprising event boundaries requires taking into account how the story developed prior to the previous sentence in setting up the context for the current sentence. This finding echoes results by Townsend (2018) that showed that surprising sentences take a long time to read because it requires changing our mental model formed from previous sentences.

F1 varies with majority agreement Since the annotations were subjective and did not always agree, we further examine our best model's performance (PREVIOUSONLY) with respect to annotation agreement. As shown in Figure 3, F1 increases with majority label agreement (Pearson's $r = 0.953$, $p < 0.05$). Such positive correlations are observed across all event boundary labels (Pearson's r = 0.869-0.994) and is especially strong for surprising event boundaries (Pearson's $r = 0.994$, $p < 0.001$). This means that most errors are made on samples that have low agreement among annotators. For example to show this contrast, after "*She and I are very close so it was great to see her marrying someone she loves*," 7 out of 8 annotators indicated that "*The most memorable moment was when I spilled champagne on my dress before the wedding*" was surprising. On the other hand, after "*It was a hot day in July that our community decided to paint a mural on an intersection for public art*," only 4 out of 8 annotators indicated that "*I had decided to volunteer to help paint.*" was surprising. The results suggest that our model performance reflects the variability and agreements in human annotations of event boundaries. We hypothesize that the event boundaries with more agreement are based on features that are shared across the annotators, such as commonsense knowledge; therefore, the model performs well in detecting those. Whereas, our model struggles with detecting event boundaries that are more subjective.

Predictive features By integrating a separate feature-based classifier, the Event Boudary Detector model allows us to examine the model parameters and determine features that are associated with surprising, expected or no event boundaries. First, we take the average of the GRU classifier weights for each of the 10 cross-validated models. Then, we plot these weights for each label in Figure 4, and summarize the findings below.

Features that relate to commonsense relations: `oEffect`, `xEffect` and `Glucose Dim-6` (caused by) are most predictive of expected event boundaries. This can indicate that events that are an effect of/caused by a prior event can be expected by annotators, as also noted by Graesser et al. (1981). An example of an expected event boundary is "*I told her we could go for coffee sometime.*", as an effect of "*We had a good time together.*" `xNeed` is least indicative of surprising event boundaries. This is likely because `xNeed` refers to what the subject needs to do before an activity, which is procedural and unlikely to cause surprise. An example is *"I was grocery shopping a few weeks ago."* which is needed before *"I had purchased my items and was leaving the store."*

Features that explain unlikely events `Realis` is highest for surprising event boundaries, suggesting that surprising event boundaries tend to contain the most concrete event-words. Surprising event boundaries also have the highest likelihood when conditioned on the story topic (`NLL_topic`) while expected events are highest when conditioned based on the topic and the previous sentence (`NLL_topic+prev`). This suggests that surprising events are often inline with the story topic but not with the previous sentence. Therefore, the low likelihood of transitioning between the previous and current sentence is a strong predictor of surprising event boundaries, in line with findings by Foster and Keane (2015) on how the difficulty of linking two adjacent events is an important factor in causing surprise.

Features that explain changes in emotional valence Compared to sentences that contain no event boundaries, sentences that contain either expected or surprising event boundaries have higher `xReact` and `oReact`, which are emotional responses either by the subject or by others to an event. For example, this is the case for the surprising and emotional event boundary "*I remember it was like the 3rd or 4th game when something bad happened..*" This suggests that event boundaries are more likely when a sentence is more emotionally charged, echoing work by Dunsmoor et al. (2018) on how event segmentation is particularly frequent when the emotion of fear is triggered.

6 Comparison with Story Cloze Test

To better understand how surprising event boundaries relate to deviation from commonsense reasoning, we compare our Event Boundary Detection Task to the ROC Story Cloze Test (Mostafazadeh et al., 2016). This test involves identifying whether a candidate ending sentence follows commonsense (*commonsense ending*) or deviates from commonsense (*nonsense ending*) given the first four sentences of a English short story. The ROC Story Cloze Test dataset contains 3142 samples with 1571 commonsense endings and 1571 nonsense endings.[3] We train a separate Event Boundary Detector model on the ROC Story Cloze Test, using the same experimental setup as for event boundary detection, except the loss function; we use the cross-entropy loss since only one label is available for each sample.[4]

	overall F1	nonsense ending F1	commonsense ending F1
Event Detector w RoBERTa			
AllToCurrent	87.9	87.8	88.0
PreviousOnly	87.6	87.3	87.8
Sequential	87.3	87.1	87.5
RoBERTa	87.7	87.6	87.8

Table 3: ROC Story Cloze Test

Performance of Event Detector on ROC Story Cloze Test Our commonsense and narrative features do not seem to significantly improve upon RoBERTa's performance in the ROC Story Cloze Test (+0.2% F1), as observed in Table 3. This indicates that detecting whether a story ending follows commonsense can be effectively approached using RoBERTa alone, setting this task might not be closely related to the Event Boundary Detection Task.

7 Conclusion

We tackle the task of identifying event boundaries in stories. We propose a model that combines predictions made using commonsense and narrative features with a RoBERTa classifier. We found that integrating commonsense and narrative features can significantly improve the prediction of surprising event boundaries through detecting violations to commonsense relations (especially relating to the absence of causality), low likelihood events, and changes in emotional valence. Our model is capable in detecting event boundaries with high annotator agreement but limited in detecting those with lower agreement. Compared to identifying commonsense and nonsense story endings in Story Cloze Test, our task is found to be only tagentially related. Our results suggest that considering commonsense knowledge and narrative features can be a promising direction towards characterizing and detecting event boundaries in stories.

[3] We use the Winter 2018 version, which contains a dev and a test set. As in previous work (Schwartz et al., 2017), we train our model on the dev portion.

[4] Training takes 20 minutes on an Nvidia P100 GPU.

References

Wasi Uddin Ahmad, Nanyun Peng, and Kai-Wei Chang. 2021. Gate: Graph attention transformer encoder for cross-lingual relation and event extraction.

Christopher Baldassano, Uri Hasson, and Kenneth A. Norman. 2018. Representation of real-world event schemas during narrative perception. *The Journal of Neuroscience*, 38(45):9689–9699.

Yonatan Bisk, Ari Holtzman, Jesse Thomason, Jacob Andreas, Yoshua Bengio, Joyce Chai, Mirella Lapata, Angeliki Lazaridou, Jonathan May, Aleksandr Nisnevich, Nicolas Pinto, and Joseph Turian. 2020. Experience grounds language. In *Proceedings of the 2020 Conference on Empirical Methods in Natural Language Processing (EMNLP)*, pages 8718–8735, Online. Association for Computational Linguistics.

Antoine Bosselut, Hannah Rashkin, Maarten Sap, Chaitanya Malaviya, Asli Çelikyilmaz, and Yejin Choi. 2019. Comet: Commonsense transformers for automatic knowledge graph construction. In *Proceedings of the 57th Annual Meeting of the Association for Computational Linguistics (ACL)*.

Luis Emilio Bruni, Sarune Baceviciute, and Mohammed Arief. 2014. Narrative cognition in interactive systems: Suspense-surprise and the p300 erp component. In *Interactive Storytelling*, pages 164–175, Cham. Springer International Publishing.

Nathanael Chambers and Dan Jurafsky. 2008. Unsupervised learning of narrative event chains. In *Proceedings of ACL-08: HLT*, pages 789–797, Columbus, Ohio. Association for Computational Linguistics.

Yubo Chen, Shulin Liu, Xiang Zhang, Kang Liu, and Jun Zhao. 2017. Automatically labeled data generation for large scale event extraction. In *Proceedings of the 55th Annual Meeting of the Association for Computational Linguistics (Volume 1: Long Papers)*, pages 409–419, Vancouver, Canada. Association for Computational Linguistics.

Jacob Devlin, Ming-Wei Chang, Kenton Lee, and Kristina Toutanova. 2019. BERT: Pre-training of deep bidirectional transformers for language understanding. In *Proceedings of the 2019 Conference of the North American Chapter of the Association for Computational Linguistics: Human Language Technologies, Volume 1 (Long and Short Papers)*, pages 4171–4186, Minneapolis, Minnesota. Association for Computational Linguistics.

Joseph E. Dunsmoor, Marijn C. W. Kroes, Caroline M. Moscatelli, Michael D. Evans, Lila Davachi, and Elizabeth A. Phelps. 2018. Event segmentation protects emotional memories from competing experiences encoded close in time. *Nature Human Behaviour*, 2(4):291–299.

Meadhbh I. Foster and Mark T. Keane. 2015. Predicting surprise judgments from explanation graphs.

Saadia Gabriel, Chandra Bhagavatula, Vered Shwartz, Ronan Le Bras, Maxwell Forbes, and Yejin Choi. 2021. Paragraph-level commonsense transformers with recurrent memory. *Proceedings of the AAAI Conference on Artificial Intelligence*, 35(14):12857–12865.

Sarik Ghazarian, Zixi Liu, Akash S M, Ralph Weischedel, Aram Galstyan, and Nanyun Peng. 2021. Plot-guided adversarial example construction for evaluating open-domain story generation. In *Proceedings of the 2021 Conference of the North American Chapter of the Association for Computational Linguistics: Human Language Technologies*, pages 4334–4344, Online. Association for Computational Linguistics.

Jonathan Gordon and Benjamin Van Durme. 2013. Reporting bias and knowledge acquisition. In *Proceedings of the 2013 Workshop on Automated Knowledge Base Construction*, AKBC '13, page 25–30, New York, NY, USA. Association for Computing Machinery.

Arthur C Graesser, Scott P Robertson, and Patricia A Anderson. 1981. Incorporating inferences in narrative representations: A study of how and why. *Cognitive Psychology*, 13(1):1–26.

Anna Jafarpour, Elizabeth A Buffalo, Robert T Knight, and Anne GE Collins. 2019a. Event segmentation reveals working memory forgetting rate. *Available at SSRN 3614120*.

Anna Jafarpour, Sandon Griffin, Jack J Lin, and Robert T Knight. 2019b. Medial orbitofrontal cortex, dorsolateral prefrontal cortex, and hippocampus differentially represent the event saliency. *Journal of cognitive neuroscience*, 31(6):874–884.

CA Kurby and JM Zacks. 2009. Segmentation in the perception and memory of events. *Trends in cognitive sciences*.

Christopher A Kurby and Jeffrey M Zacks. 2008. Segmentation in the perception and memory of events. *Trends in cognitive sciences*, 12(2):72–79.

Qi Li, Heng Ji, and Liang Huang. 2013. Joint event extraction via structured prediction with global features. In *Proceedings of the 51st Annual Meeting of the Association for Computational Linguistics (Volume 1: Long Papers)*, pages 73–82, Sofia, Bulgaria. Association for Computational Linguistics.

Yinhan Liu, Myle Ott, Naman Goyal, Jingfei Du, Mandar Joshi, Danqi Chen, Omer Levy, Mike Lewis, Luke Zettlemoyer, and Veselin Stoyanov. 2019. Roberta: A robustly optimized bert pretraining approach.

Lara Martin, Prithviraj Ammanabrolu, Xinyu Wang, William Hancock, Shruti Singh, Brent Harrison, and Mark Riedl. 2018. Event representations for automated story generation with deep neural nets. *Proceedings of the AAAI Conference on Artificial Intelligence*, 32(1).

Quinn McNemar. 1947. Note on the sampling error of the difference between correlated proportions or percentages. *Psychometrika*, 12(2):153–157.

Nasrin Mostafazadeh, Nathanael Chambers, Xiaodong He, Devi Parikh, Dhruv Batra, Lucy Vanderwende, Pushmeet Kohli, and James Allen. 2016. A corpus and cloze evaluation for deeper understanding of commonsense stories. In *Proceedings of the 2016 Conference of the North American Chapter of the Association for Computational Linguistics: Human Language Technologies*, pages 839–849, San Diego, California. Association for Computational Linguistics.

Nasrin Mostafazadeh, Aditya Kalyanpur, Lori Moon, David Buchanan, Lauren Berkowitz, Or Biran, and Jennifer Chu-Carroll. 2020. GLUCOSE: GeneraLized and COntextualized story explanations. In *Proceedings of the 2020 Conference on Empirical Methods in Natural Language Processing (EMNLP)*, pages 4569–4586, Online. Association for Computational Linguistics.

Aida Nematzadeh, Kaylee Burns, Erin Grant, Alison Gopnik, and Tom Griffiths. 2018. Evaluating theory of mind in question answering. In *Proceedings of the 2018 Conference on Empirical Methods in Natural Language Processing*, pages 2392–2400, Brussels, Belgium. Association for Computational Linguistics.

Takaki Otake, Sho Yokoi, Naoya Inoue, Ryo Takahashi, Tatsuki Kuribayashi, and Kentaro Inui. 2020. Modeling event salience in narratives via barthes' cardinal functions. In *Proceedings of the 28th International Conference on Computational Linguistics*, pages 1784–1794, Barcelona, Spain (Online). International Committee on Computational Linguistics.

Jessica Ouyang and Kathleen McKeown. 2015. Modeling reportable events as turning points in narrative. In *Proceedings of the 2015 Conference on Empirical Methods in Natural Language Processing*, pages 2149–2158, Lisbon, Portugal. Association for Computational Linguistics.

Ellie Pavlick and Tom Kwiatkowski. 2019. Inherent disagreements in human textual inferences. *Transactions of the Association for Computational Linguistics*, 7:677–694.

Kyle A. Pettijohn and Gabriel A. Radvansky. 2016. Narrative event boundaries, reading times, and expectation. *Memory & Cognition*, 44(7):1064–1075.

Alec Radford, Jeff Wu, Rewon Child, David Luan, Dario Amodei, and Ilya Sutskever. 2019. Language models are unsupervised multitask learners.

Gabriel A. Radvansky, Andrea K. Tamplin, Joseph Armendarez, and Alexis N. Thompson. 2014. Different kinds of causality in event cognition. *Discourse Processes*, 51(7):601–618.

Hannah Rashkin, Asli Celikyilmaz, Yejin Choi, and Jianfeng Gao. 2020. PlotMachines: Outline-conditioned generation with dynamic plot state tracking. In *Proceedings of the 2020 Conference on Empirical Methods in Natural Language Processing (EMNLP)*, pages 4274–4295, Online. Association for Computational Linguistics.

Hannah Rashkin, Maarten Sap, Emily Allaway, Noah A. Smith, and Yejin Choi. 2018. Event2mind: Commonsense inference on events, intents, and reactions. In *ACL*.

Nils Reimers and Iryna Gurevych. 2019. Sentence-bert: Sentence embeddings using siamese bert-networks. In *Proceedings of the 2019 Conference on Empirical Methods in Natural Language Processing*. Association for Computational Linguistics.

Corby Rosset. 2020. Turing-nlg: A 17-billion-parameter language model by microsoft.

Marie-Laure Ryan. 2010. Narratology and cognitive science: A problematic relation. *Style*, 44(4):469–495.

Maarten Sap, Eric Horvitz, Yejin Choi, Noah A Smith, and James W Pennebaker. 2020. Recollection versus imagination: Exploring human memory and cognition via neural language models. In *ACL*.

Maarten Sap, Anna Jafarpour, Yejin Choi, Noah A. Smith, James W. Pennebaker, and Eric Horvitz. 2022. Computational lens on cognition: Study of autobiographical versus imagined stories with large-scale language models.

Maarten Sap, Ronan Le Bras, Emily Allaway, Chandra Bhagavatula, Nicholas Lourie, Hannah Rashkin, Brendan Roof, Noah A. Smith, and Yejin Choi. 2019a. Atomic: An atlas of machine commonsense for if-then reasoning. *Proceedings of the AAAI Conference on Artificial Intelligence*, 33(01):3027–3035.

Maarten Sap, Hannah Rashkin, Derek Chen, Ronan Le Bras, and Yejin Choi. 2019b. Social IQa: Commonsense reasoning about social interactions. In *Proceedings of the 2019 Conference on Empirical Methods in Natural Language Processing and the 9th International Joint Conference on Natural Language Processing (EMNLP-IJCNLP)*, pages 4463–4473, Hong Kong, China. Association for Computational Linguistics.

R.C. Schank and R. Abelson. 1977. *Scripts, Plans, Goals, and Understanding*. Hillsdale, NJ: Earlbaum Assoc.

Roy Schwartz, Maarten Sap, Ioannis Konstas, Li Zilles, Yejin Choi, and Noah A Smith. 2017. The effect of different writing tasks on linguistic style: A case study of the roc story cloze task. In *CoNLL*.

Matthew Sims, Jong Ho Park, and David Bamman. 2019. Literary event detection. In *Proceedings of the 57th Annual Meeting of the Association for Computational Linguistics*, pages 3623–3634, Florence, Italy. Association for Computational Linguistics.

Kaitao Song, Xu Tan, Tao Qin, Jianfeng Lu, and Tie-Yan Liu. 2020. Mpnet: Masked and permuted pre-training for language understanding. *arXiv preprint arXiv:2004.09297*.

David J. Townsend. 2018. Stage salience and situational likelihood in the formation of situation models during sentence comprehension. *Lingua*, 206:1–20.

Ercenur Ünal, Yue Ji, and Anna Papafragou. 2019. From event representation to linguistic meaning. *Topics in Cognitive Science*, 13(1):224–242.

Christopher Walker, Stephanie Strassel, Julie Medero, and Kazuaki Maeda. 2006. Ace 2005 multilingual training corpus.

David Wilmot and Frank Keller. 2021. Memory and knowledge augmented language models for inferring salience in long-form stories. In *Proceedings of the 2021 Conference on Empirical Methods in Natural Language Processing*, pages 851–865, Online and Punta Cana, Dominican Republic. Association for Computational Linguistics.

Timothy D. Wilson and Daniel T. Gilbert. 2008. Explaining away: A model of affective adaptation. *Perspectives on Psychological Science*, 3(5):370–386. PMID: 26158955.

Thomas Wolf, Lysandre Debut, Victor Sanh, Julien Chaumond, Clement Delangue, Anthony Moi, Pierric Cistac, Tim Rault, Rémi Louf, Morgan Funtowicz, Joe Davison, Sam Shleifer, Patrick von Platen, Clara Ma, Yacine Jernite, Julien Plu, Canwen Xu, Teven Le Scao, Sylvain Gugger, Mariama Drame, Quentin Lhoest, and Alexander M. Rush. 2020. Transformers: State-of-the-art natural language processing. In *Proceedings of the 2020 Conference on Empirical Methods in Natural Language Processing: System Demonstrations*, pages 38–45, Online. Association for Computational Linguistics.

Lili Yao, Nanyun Peng, Weischedel Ralph, Kevin Knight, Dongyan Zhao, and Rui Yan. 2019. Plan-and-write: Towards better automatic storytelling. In *The Thirty-Third AAAI Conference on Artificial Intelligence (AAAI-19)*.

Jeffrey M. Zacks. 2020. Event perception and memory. *Annual Review of Psychology*, 71(1):165–191. PMID: 31905113.

Jeffrey M Zacks, Nicole K Speer, Khena M Swallow, Todd S Braver, and Jeremy R Reynolds. 2007. Event perception: a mind-brain perspective. *Psychological bulletin*, 133(2):273.

A Appendix

A.1 Atomic relations training details

We used the train/dev/test splits from the original Atomic dataset (Sap et al., 2019a). Negative samples are created by matching a Atomic event node to a corresponding tail event node from another sample based on the relationship involved. Sepcifically, negative sampling was performed on groups (['xWant', 'oWant', 'xNeed', 'xIntent'],['xReact', 'oReact', 'xAttr'],['xEffect', 'oEffect']) given that the tail event nodes in each group are more similar, creating more discriminating negative samples, as inspired by Sap et al. (2019b). One negative sample is introduced every nine positive samples, since there are nine labels. We used a learning rate of 1e-4, batch size of 64, 8 epochs and AdamW optimizer. Training took 18 hours on a Nvidia P100 GPU.

A.2 Glucose relations training details

Because the Glucose dataset (Mostafazadeh et al., 2020) was not split initially, we randomly split the dataset into train/dev/test splits based on a 80/10/10 ratio. For each sample in Glucose, annotations share similar head event nodes in Dim-1 to 5 and similar tail event nodes in Dim-6 to 10. Therefore, our negative sampling strategy for Dim-1 to 5 involves randomly choosing a tail node from Dim-6 to 10 and vice-versa. As a result, one negative sample is introduced every five samples. During training, we used a learning rate of 1e-4, batch size of 64, 8 epochs and AdamW optimizer. Training took 15 hours on a Nvidia P100 GPU.

A.3 Realis training details

We used the train/dev/test split from the Realis dataset (Sims et al., 2019). During training, we used the AdamW optimizer, a learning rate of 2e-5, 3 epochs and batch size of 4, as inspired by (Sap et al., 2020). Training took 1 hour on a Nvidia P100 GPU.

A.4 Sequentiality experimental details

GPT2-small was accessed from HuggingFace Transformers library and used without further fine-tuning. It has 125M parameters, a context window of 1024, hidden state dimension of 768, 12 heads and dropout of 0.1.

A.5 SimGen experimental details

We used the Turing-NLG model without further fine-tuning. The model has 17B and we used it with top-p sampling (top-p=0.85), temperature=1.0 and max sequence length of 64 tokens. MPnet-base model was accessed from the Sentence-BERT library (Reimers and Gurevych, 2019) and used without further fine-tuning.

A.6 Event Boundary Detection Model training details

AdamW optimizer was used with $\alpha = 5 * 10^{-6}$, following a uniform search using F1 as the criterion at intervals of $\{2.5, 5, 7.5, 10\} * 10^{n}; -6 \leq n \leq -3$. Learning rate was linearly decayed (8 epochs) with 100 warm-up steps. Batch size of 16 was used. Validation was done every 0.25 epochs during training. Training each model took around 30 minutes on an Nvidia P100 GPU.

Compositional Generalization for Kinship Prediction through Data Augmentation

Kangda Wei Sayan Ghosh Shashank Srivastava
UNC Chapel Hill
kangda@live.unc.edu, {sayghosh, ssrivastava}@cs.unc.edu

Abstract

Transformer-based models have shown promising performance in numerous NLP tasks. However, recent work has shown the limitation of such models in showing compositional generalization, which requires models to generalize to novel compositions of known concepts. In this work, we explore two strategies for compositional generalization on the task of kinship prediction from stories: (1) data augmentation and (2) predicting and using intermediate structured representation (in form of kinship graphs). Our experiments show that data augmentation boosts generalization performance by around 20% on average relative to a baseline model from prior work not using these strategies. However, predicting and using intermediate kinship graphs leads to a deterioration in the generalization of kinship prediction by around 50% on average relative to models that only leverage data augmentation.

1 Introduction

Transformer-based large language models (Vaswani et al., 2017) have achieved state-of-the-art results on numerous NLP tasks such as question answering, reading comprehension, relational reasoning, etc. that require both syntactic and semantic understanding of language. However, recent works (Bahdanau et al., 2018; Lake and Baroni, 2018; Gururangan et al., 2018; Kaushik and Lipton, 2018) have shown that these transformer-based models have their limitations when it comes to tasks that require compositional generalization as they often perform surface-level reasoning instead of understanding the underlying concepts and learning to generalize and reason over them. On the other hand, neural models that encode the structure of the data (such as Graph Attention Networks (Veličković et al., 2017)) instead of consuming it in an unstructured format

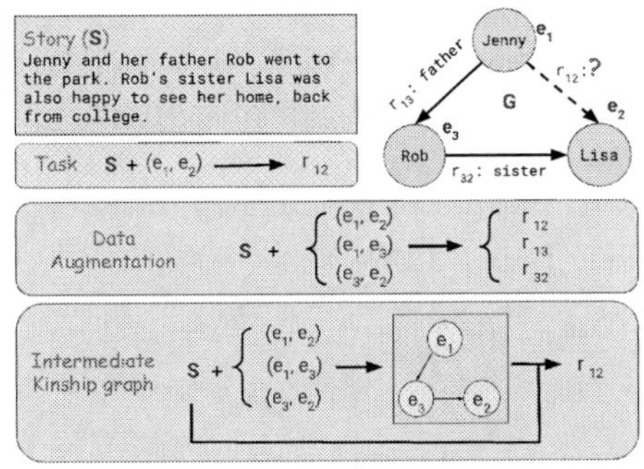

Figure 1: To improve the compositional generalization of models for the task of kinship prediction between a pair of queried entities (e.g. predicting the relation r_{12} given the entities e_1 and e_2) from a story (S) we present two strategies (1) data augmentation and (2) predicting and using intermediate structured representation in form of kinship graphs. For data augmentation (first strategy), we utilize the existing ground truth graph (G) to generate more pairs of target relations and query entities (such as predicting r_{13} using e_1 and e_3) that do not need compositional inference to obtain the answer. In our second strategy, using our augmented data we predict an intermediate kinship graph and reason over it jointly with the story to predict the relation between the queried pair of entities.

show better compositional generalization (Sinha et al., 2019).

In this work, we explore two strategies to improve the compositional generalization of models for the task of kinship prediction from stories. In our first strategy, we explore the utility of data augmentation towards compositional generalization. Recent works have shown data augmentation to be an effective strategy in improving model performance on different NLP tasks such as Neural Machine Translation (Fernando and Ranathunga, 2022), semantic parsing (Yang et al., 2022), and text summarization (Wan and Bansal, 2022). Our data augmentation strategy focuses on improving a model's ability to extract relations that are explicitly mentioned in the text. In our second strategy,

Proceedings of the 3rd Wordplay: When Language Meets Games Workshop (Wordplay 2022), pages 13 - 19
July 15, 2022 ©2022 Association for Computational Linguistics

we explore the utility of predicting an intermediate structured representation of the story (as a kinship graph) and then jointly reasoning over it along with the story text for the task of kinship prediction. Figure 1 provides an example of this task and also illustrates the two strategies. The strategies are explained in detail in §3.

We evaluate the utility of our strategies on a kinship prediction benchmark, CLUTRR (Sinha et al., 2019). Overall, we find data augmentation is helpful and boosts the generalization performance (accuracy of predicting correct relation) by around 20% on average relative to a baseline not using these strategies. However, using intermediate kinship graphs deteriorates generalization performance by almost 50% as compared to the model that only uses data augmentation. Our code is available at: `https://github.com/WeiKangda/data-aug-clutrr`.

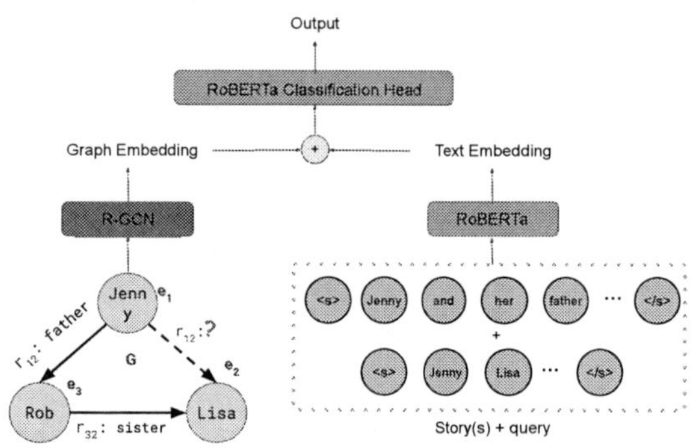

Figure 2: SSD model illustration: first obtain the graph embedding and text embedding separately using R-GCN and RoBERTa respectively, then adding the embeddings together and feeding through a classification layer to get the final output.

2 Problem Setup

Each example in CLUTTR (Sinha et al., 2019) is a tuple of the form (S, G, e_1, e_2), where S represents the story/passage describing the entities (fictional characters) and relations between them, G represents the kinship graph, e_1 and e_2 represent the pair of query entities (whose relationship is being queried). To aid clarity on these notations, we have illustrated the values of (S, G, e_1, e_2) corresponding to our running example in Figure 1. Further, each kinship graph can be considered to be a collection of entity nodes (E) and relation edges (R) (as illustrated in Figure 1), where $E = (e_1, e_2, e_3)$ and $R = (r_{12}, r_{13}, r_{32})$. Note that the kinship graph mentions only the relationships clearly stated in the story. For example, in Figure 1, the entity pairs (e_1, e_3) and (e_3, e_2) are explicitly mentioned in story S. The learning task is to predict the relationship between the two query entities. This is framed as a classification task over 20 possible relationship types in the dataset. The number of composition operations/steps required to infer the relationship between the query entities is denoted by k. For example, in figure 1, $k = 2$ for inferring the relationship between e_1 and e_2 as there are 2 composition operations needed to get the final result.

In this work, we empirically evaluate the utility of data augmentation and intermediate structured representations towards compositional generalization for the task of kinship prediction from a story. Next, we formally describe our model, `SSD`, where `SSD` stands for Systematic Compositional Generalization with Symbolic Representation and Data Augmentation for Kinship Prediction.

3 Method

We first describe our base model followed by a description of two strategies explored in this work - (1) data augmentation and (2) predicting and using intermediate kinship graphs.

Our base model, `SSD` (base) is adapted from the RoBERTa-based (Liu et al., 2019) baseline presented in Sinha et al. (2019). However, different from Sinha et al. (2019) we allow finetuning of the RoBERTa transformer layers. Grounding in the running example, given S, e_1, and e_2, `SSD` (base) predicts the relation r_{12} between e_1 and e_2 using the following three steps:

1. Obtaining story representation: This is the `[CLS]` representation by doing a forward pass of RoBERTa on the story, S.
2. Obtaining entity representations: During training, each entity (such as e_1, e_2, etc.) is replaced by a unique number in the story (following Sinha et al. (2019)). We obtain the representation for each entity by averaging the tokens from the last transformer layer of RoBERTa corresponding to the positions where the entity appeared in the story.
3. Classifier for predicting relation: This is a multi-class classification task (with total number of classes as the number of relationships possible in the dataset) using a linear classifier that takes as input the concatenation of representations of

the story and two query entities.

3.1 Data Augmentation

For each example in our training set, we augment the training set further by considering the pairs of entities for which the relation is explicitly mentioned in the story thus requiring no composition operations. We illustrate this data augmentation procedure using our running example in figure 1. We add the query entity pairs (e_1, e_3) and (e_2, e_3) in the training set as the relationships for these pair of entities are explicitly mentioned in the story. To predict the relation between the pair of entities mentioned in a query, the model has to operate in two stages, (1) extracting the relations mentioned explicitly in the story and (2) performing compositional reasoning over the extracted relations. This data augmentation procedure helps to ensure that the model becomes better at extracting the relations that are mentioned explicitly in the story, thus not propagating any error from the relation extraction stage to the compositional reasoning stage for predicting the target relation between the queried pair of entities. This model is denoted as SSD (data aug) henceforth. For inference using SSD (data aug) one needs to provide all the pairs of query entities whose relations can be extracted directly from the text of the story in addition to the actual pair of query entities.

3.2 Intermediate Kinship Graphs

Prior work has found models using structured representation of stories in form of kinship graphs perform better than transformer models trained only on stories for this task. However, it is unreasonable to assume that we will always have access to gold kinship graphs for the task of kinship prediction from narratives or stories during inference. Hence, we empirically evaluate the utility of predicting an intermediate kinship graph and then jointly reasoning over the predicted graph and the input story to predict the relation between the queried pair of entities. We illustrate our strategy using the running example in figure 1. We form the intermediate kinship graph, G' by predicting the relations between the entities whose relations are explicitly mentioned in the story. We predict the relations to form this intermediate graph by using a linear layer over representations of the story and the pair of query entities obtained using a RoBERTa model.

Next, we obtain two representations of the target relation based on (1) text: using linear layer over representations of the story and the pair of query entities obtained using a RoBERTa model and (2) graph: using linear layer over representations of kinship graph and query entities obtained using R-GCN (Schlichtkrull et al., 2017) (see Appendix for details). We concatenate these two target relation representations and use another linear layer to predict the target relation. This model is denoted as SSD (graph) henceforth.

Similar to SSD (data aug), for inference using SSD (graph) one needs to provide all the pairs of query entities whose relations can be extracted directly from the text of the story in addition to the actual pair of query entities.

4 Experiments and Results

All models are trained using cross-entropy loss. Every model is trained with 40 epochs and a learning rate of 5e-6.

4.1 Baseline and Evaluation Metrics

We consider the RoBERTa-based model in Sinha et al. (2019) as our baseline. Note that in the baseline the transformer layers of RoBERTa are not finetuned. For all our experiments we report the accuracy of predicting the relation between the queried pair of entities. Further, following Sinha et al. (2019), we report the accuracy over multiple test sets, where each test set is characterized by k, the number of composition operations/steps required to find the relation between the queried pair of entities. For example, in figure 1, the number of composition steps (k) is 2. In test sets of CLUTRR, k varies from 2 to 10.

4.2 Evaluating compositional generalization

Figure 3 shows the accuracy of different variants of SSD on the test sets of CLUTRR. We consider two settings, where SSD is trained on data with (1) $k = 2,3$ and (2) $k = 2,3,4$ Irrespective of the training data complexity (in terms of k), we observe that SSD (data aug) outperforms baseline. Notably, we see improvements even when $k = 10$ during test showing the utility of data augmentation for improving the generalizability of the models.

While data augmentation shows promise, we do not see any improvements when predicting and reasoning jointly over the intermediate kinship graph. Rather, the performance of the models drop significantly when we predict the relation conditioned on the story and the intermediate kinship graph. This

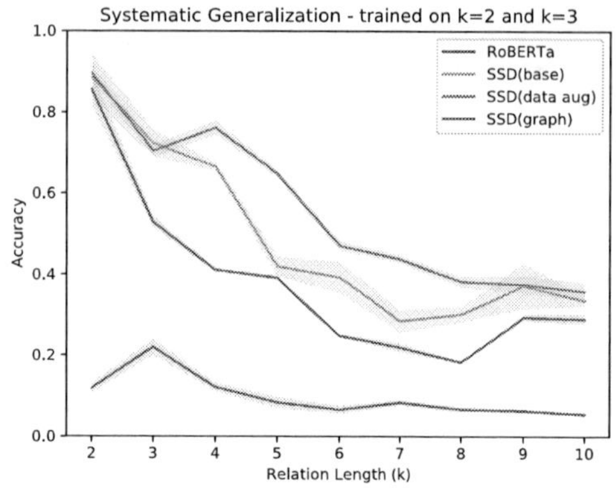

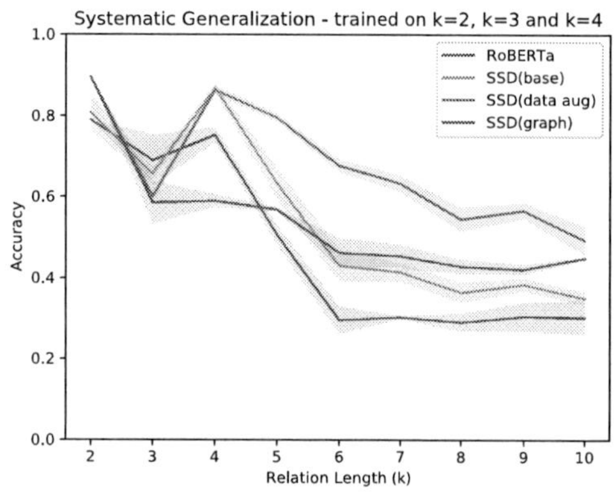

Figure 3: compositional generalization performance of different models when trained on $k = 2, 3$ and $k = 2, 3, 4$. Our presented strategies boost accuracy even when the number of composition steps (k) is 10.

is counter-intuitive as we hypothesized the intermediate kinship graph (which is structured) would aid the model further in making compositions. As one of the possible reasons for this, we hypothesize that our method of fusing representations from two modalities, story and graph, might be sub-optimal that results in the failure. Future work can explicitly look into devising better techniques for this fusion.

Generalization with noisy inputs: We also evaluate the models with noisy train and noisy test sets of CLUTRR following Sinha et al. (2019). We explore the following three noisy data settings shown in Figure 4:

- Supporting facts: There are two reasoning paths that can lead to the correct answer p_c and p_n. These two paths has the same beginning and ending nodes but p_c is shorter than p_n (smaller k).

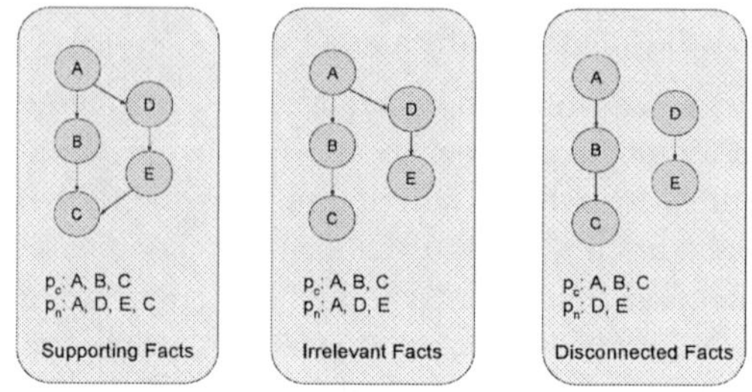

Figure 4: Categories of Noisy Inputs. The query is finding the relationship between entity A and entity C.

- Irrelevant facts: p_n, the path that contains the irrelevant facts, shares the same beginning node with p_c which leads to the correct answer. p_n can be seen as a branch of the graph that doesn't lead to the correct answer.
- Disconnected facts: p_n, which is the path that contains the disconnected facts, can be treated as another graph that is disconnected from the main story that contains the reasoning path p_c, which leads to the correct answer.

Table 1 shows the result of different SSD variants when evaluated on the noisy test sets. The model performance decreases as the number of deduction steps required (k) increases, which is consistent with other experiments' results. We can also notice that the models, SSD (base) and SSD (graph), tend to perform better with graphs that contain supporting facts, irrelevant facts, and disconnected facts compared to graphs that are free of noise but require the same number of composition operations (k) to predict the target relation. This shows that SSD is good at identifying useful and relevant information from the graph and extra information from the noisy inputs improves the models' performance.

4.3 Varying the amount of additional annotation

For data augmentation and also for predicting the intermediate kinship graphs we need additional annotation to identify entity pairs whose relationship is explicitly mentioned in the text. While there can be heuristic approaches to estimate such entity pairs (for example, set of all distinct entity pairs that appear in the same sentence), in this work we re-purpose the gold kinship graphs to get this annotation. Realistically, having gold kinship graphs

Model	Train Set	Test Set	Accuracy	Test Set	Accuracy	Test Set	Accuracy	Test Set	Accuracy	Test Set	Accuracy	Average Accuracy
SSD (base)	1.2,1.3	1.2	82.2%	1.3	61.0%	2.3	75.9%	3.3	76.5%	4.3	69.6%	73.0%
	2.2,2.3	2.2	93.4%	2.3	84.1%	1.3	61.3%	3.3	75.9%	4.3	72.4%	77.4%
	3.2,3.3	3.2	97.4%	3.3	72.4%	1.3	56.5%	2.3	79.9%	4.3	69.6%	75.2%
	4.2,4.3	4.2	62.5%	4.3	68.9%	1.3	55.3%	2.3	77.1%	3.3	72.9%	67.3%
SSD (graph)	1.2,1.3	1.2	88.8%	1.3	43.3%	2.3	69.6%	3.3	69.5%	4.3	58.3%	65.9%
	2.2,2.3	2.2	92.1%	2.3	75.7%	1.3	42.7%	3.3	70.8%	4.3	54.1%	67.1%
	3.2,3.3	3.2	97.4%	3.3	64.3%	1.3	36.8%	2.3	71.9%	4.3	50.0%	64.1%
	4.2,4.3	4.2	68.4%	4.3	58.9%	1.3	43.3%	2.3	72.4%	3.3	69.3%	62.5%

Table 1: Testing SSD (base) and SSD (graph) performance when training on story graphs with or without noisy inputs. The integer after symbol . represents the number of steps required to infer the relationship between the query entities, which is k as mentioned section 2.1, and the integer before the symbol . has the following meaning provided by the original CLUTRR paper (Sinha et al., 2019): 1=free of noise; 2=with supporting facts; 3 = with irrelevant facts; 4 = with disconnected facts.

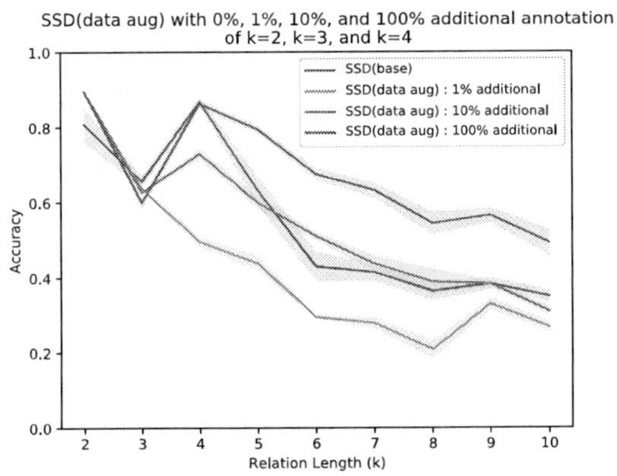

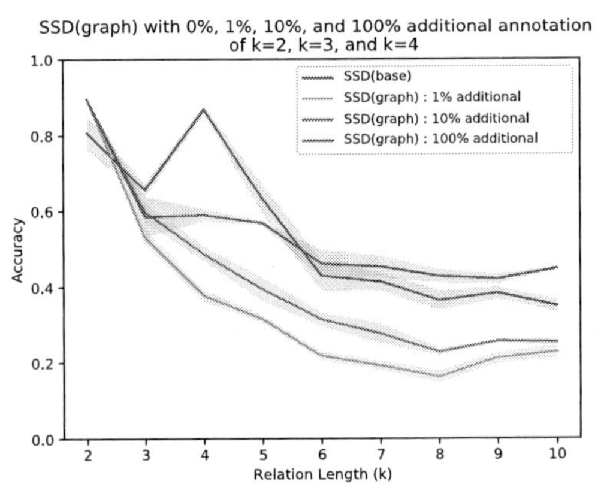

Figure 5: Comparison of model performance when additional supervision (through data augmentation and intermediate kinship graphs) is only available for 1% and 10% of the data and the rest is trained without additional supervision.

for all the training data might not be feasible. In this section we empirically explore how much performance improvement we would achieve if we had access to only 1% (and 10%) of gold kinship graphs to obtain the additional annotation of entity pairs for data augmentation.

Figure 5 our assumption is reasonable as the performance of only allowing additional supervision for 10% of the training data achieves decent accuracy.

4.4 Low data regime

Next, we study the effect of reducing the size of training dataset and evaluate the effectiveness of our strategies under this setting. We reduce the training data size gradually by an order of 10 and form two smaller training splits with sizes around 1000 and 100 samples. Figure 6 and Figure 7 shows the results of our proposed model on the standard (no-noise) CLUTRR test datasets as we reduce the overall size of our training datasets with k=2,3 and k=2,3,4 respectively. We find that even in low data regime data augmentation leads to improvements.

5 Conclusion

In this paper, we present SSD to empirically evaluate the utility of two strategies (1) data augmentation and (2) predicting and using intermediate kinship graphs, towards compositional generalization of transformer-based models for the task of kinship prediction from a story. While data augmentation boosts the performance of our model, using intermediate kinship graphs leads to a downfall in the overall performance. Data augmentation is fruitful even when additional supervision in form of ground-truth kinship graphs is present for a limited set of examples. Future work can explore better methods to fuse the information from the intermediate kinship graph and the story instead of simple concatenation as done in this work.

References

Dzmitry Bahdanau, Shikhar Murty, Michael Noukhovitch, Thien Huu Nguyen, Harm de Vries, and Aaron Courville. 2018. Systematic generaliza-

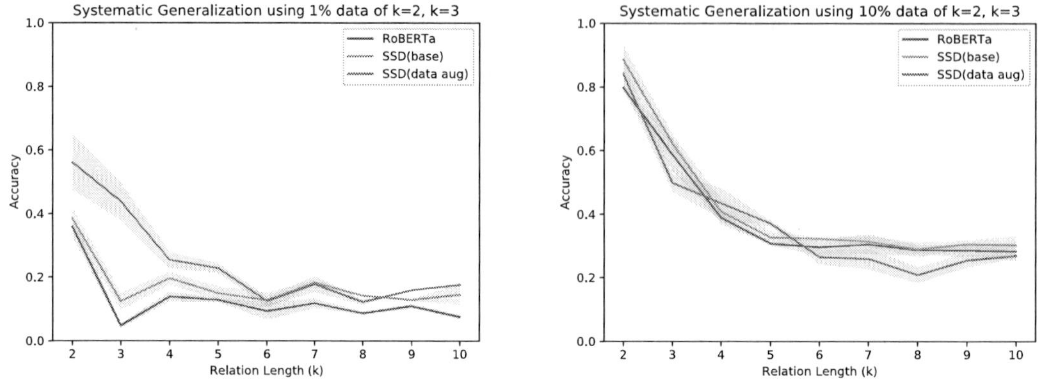

Figure 6: Low data regime performance of settings for RoBERTa when trained on k=2,3. Use of augmented data from the ground-truth kinship graph boosts accuracy even when the overall size of the training data is reduced.

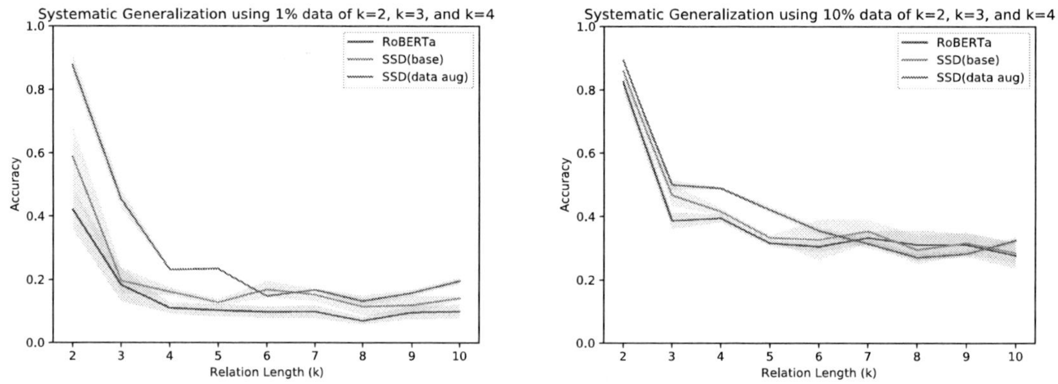

Figure 7: Low data regime performance of settings for RoBERTa when trained on k=2,3,4. Use of augmented data from the ground-truth kinship graph boosts accuracy even when the overall size of the training data is reduced.

tion: what is required and can it be learned? *arXiv preprint arXiv:1811.12889*.

Aloka Fernando and Surangika Ranathunga. 2022. Data augmentation to address out-of-vocabulary problem in low-resource sinhala-english neural machine translation.

Suchin Gururangan, Swabha Swayamdipta, Omer Levy, Roy Schwartz, Samuel R Bowman, and Noah A Smith. 2018. Annotation artifacts in natural language inference data. *arXiv preprint arXiv:1803.02324*.

Divyansh Kaushik and Zachary C Lipton. 2018. How much reading does reading comprehension require? a critical investigation of popular benchmarks. *arXiv preprint arXiv:1808.04926*.

Brenden Lake and Marco Baroni. 2018. Generalization without systematicity: On the compositional skills of sequence-to-sequence recurrent networks. In *International conference on machine learning*, pages 2873–2882. PMLR.

Yinhan Liu, Myle Ott, Naman Goyal, Jingfei Du, Mandar Joshi, Danqi Chen, Omer Levy, Mike Lewis, Luke Zettlemoyer, and Veselin Stoyanov. 2019. Roberta: A robustly optimized bert pretraining approach.

Michael Schlichtkrull, Thomas N. Kipf, Peter Bloem, Rianne van den Berg, Ivan Titov, and Max Welling. 2017. Modeling relational data with graph convolutional networks.

Koustuv Sinha, Shagun Sodhani, Jin Dong, Joelle Pineau, and William L. Hamilton. 2019. CLUTRR: A diagnostic benchmark for inductive reasoning from text. In *Proceedings of the 2019 Conference on Empirical Methods in Natural Language Processing and the 9th International Joint Conference on Natural Language Processing (EMNLP-IJCNLP)*, pages 4506–4515, Hong Kong, China. Association for Computational Linguistics.

Rupesh Kumar Srivastava, Klaus Greff, and Jürgen Schmidhuber. 2015. Highway networks. *CoRR*, abs/1505.00387.

Ashish Vaswani, Noam Shazeer, Niki Parmar, Jakob Uszkoreit, Llion Jones, Aidan N. Gomez, Lukasz Kaiser, and Illia Polosukhin. 2017. Attention is all you need.

Petar Veličković, Guillem Cucurull, Arantxa Casanova, Adriana Romero, Pietro Lio, and Yoshua Bengio. 2017. Graph attention networks. *arXiv preprint arXiv:1710.10903*.

David Wan and Mohit Bansal. 2022. Factpegasus: Factuality-aware pre-training and fine-tuning for abstractive summarization.

Kevin Yang, Olivia Deng, Charles Chen, Richard Shin, Subhro Roy, and Benjamin Van Durme. 2022. Addressing resource and privacy constraints in semantic parsing through data augmentation.

Appendix

A Description of models used to encode and reason over the intermediate kinship graph

A.1 R-GCN

The formula for Relational-Graph Conventional Networks we used is:

$$h_i^{l+1} = \sigma(W_0^l h_i^l + \sum_{r \in R} \sum_{j \in N_i^r} \frac{1}{C_i^r} W_r^l h_j^l) \quad (1)$$

where $W_0^l h_i^l$ gives special treatment to self connection, r represents the relation type, j represents the neighbor nodes of node i with relation r, and W_r^l is the projection matrix for each relation type. In our setting, we have three R-GCN (Schlichtkrull et al., 2017) layers. h is the hidden representation of an entity in the graph and r is a kinship-relation type that belongs to set R, which contains all possible relations.

A.2 Highway Connection

We utilize highway connections (Srivastava et al., 2015) between R-GCN (Schlichtkrull et al., 2017)layers:

$$g = Sigmoid(W_{hw}(\hat{h_i})) \quad (2a)$$

$$h_i^{l+1} = g \odot \hat{h_i} + (1-g) \odot h_i^l \quad (2b)$$

where W_{hw} is a linear layer, and $\odot$ denotes element-wise multiplication. h_i^l is the entity representation of the nodes in the graph from the previous layer, and $\hat{h_i}$ is the entity representation of the node in the graph acquire by passing h_i^l to a R-GCN (Schlichtkrull et al., 2017) layer.

How to be Helpful on Online Support Forums?

Zhilin Wang
University of Cambridge and Nvidia
zhilinw@nvidia.com

Pablo Torres
University of Cambridge
pelt2@cam.ac.uk

Abstract

Internet forums such as Reddit offer people a platform to ask for advice when they encounter various issues at work, school or in relationships. Telling helpful comments apart from unhelpful comments to these advice-seeking posts can help people and dialogue agents to become more helpful in offering advice. We propose a dataset that contains both helpful and unhelpful comments in response to such requests. We then relate helpfulness to the closely related construct of empathy. Finally, we analyze the language features that are associated with helpful and unhelpful comments.

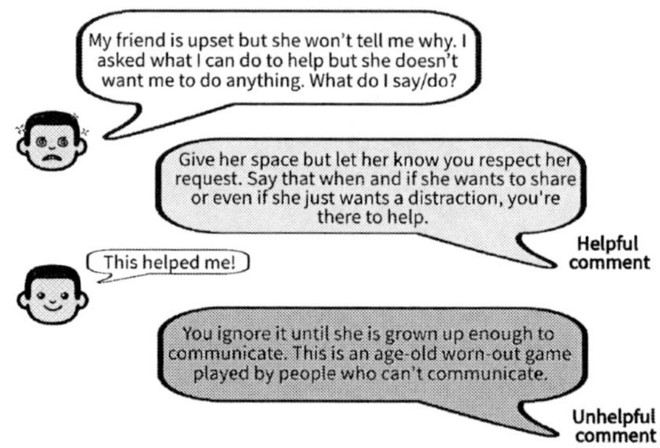

Figure 1: Examples of helpful and un-helpful comments to a help-seeking post. "Helped" is a magic word for labelling the response.

1 Introduction

When people encounter issues in their lives (such as problems with family and friends, difficulties at school/work as well as troubles in pursuing one's interests and hobbies), many seek for advice in order to solve these problems. Some ask for such advice on internet forums, such as the r/Advice subreddit[1]. Other users can then comment on these posts to attempt to help the post authors.

While many users can actively offer help, not all of them will be seen as helpful by the user asking for advice. Examples of a helpful and an unhelpful comment are presented in Figure 1 to show their contrast. In order to support people and dialogue agents to be more effective in offering helpful comments, a critical first step is to understand what makes these comments helpful. We make use of a feedback system on r/Advice that labels comments based on whether the original post author finds comments to be helpful. Based on this feedback system, we introduce a new dataset of comments, labelled with their binary helpfulness.

Helpfulness has been extensively studied based on exchanges in online support communities (Chuang and Yang, 2012; Schotanus-Dijkstra et al., 2014; Paulus and Varga, 2015; Subramani and O'Connor, 2018; McKiernan et al., 2018; Green et al., 2020). These studies found that helpfulness is associated with various characteristics such as emotional warmth, relevant knowledge, willingness to understand, empowering choice, active listening as well as sharing of similar experiences. However, these studies are solely based on qualitative interpretations and have thus far not sought to associate language features with helpfulness. To overcome this limitation, we seek to identify words that are most positively and negatively associated with helpfulness, and relate these words to characteristics of helpfulness from prior literature.

Helpfulness is closely related to empathy, as they share many characteristics such as being emotionally warm and compassionate; accepting others' frame of reference, and practising active listening (Davis, 1983; Baron-Cohen and Wheelwright, 2004; Zhou et al., 2003). We show that people's average helpfulness across all of their comments correlates with their measured empathy score. We also relate our study to literature on the language features that are associated with empathy (Sharma et al., 2020; Xiao et al., 2015; Gibson et al., 2015)

[1]https://www.reddit.com/r/Advice/

Proceedings of the 3rd Wordplay: When Language Meets Games Workshop (Wordplay 2022), pages 20 - 28
July 15, 2022

and show that there is a great overlap among their language features.

Our key contributions are:

1. We introduce and plan to openly release a novel dataset containing helpful and unhelpful comments in response to posts seeking for advice on life issues.

2. We relate helpfulness in comments that respond to posts seeking for advice on life issues to empathy.

3. We analyze the language features that are associated with helpful and unhelpful comments.

2 Related Work

Helpfulness on Online Support Communities Helpfulness has been studied in online support communities where peers can offer help and support to one another. These communities often center around a shared life situation such as chronic health conditions (Subramani and O'Connor, 2018; Green et al., 2020) and family bereavement (Schotanus-Dijkstra et al., 2014; Paulus and Varga, 2015). Several factors were emphasized in common: Peers were found more helpful when they are emotionally warm and compassionate, give others choice on a solution, willing to accept others' perspectives and experiences, practice active listening - by paraphrasing, asking questions and reflecting feelings, give pertinent advice/insights to help others to solve their problem, as well as share similar experiences (Chuang and Yang, 2012; Schotanus-Dijkstra et al., 2014; Paulus and Varga, 2015; Subramani and O'Connor, 2018; McKiernan et al., 2018; Green et al., 2020). While there has been significant work on what people find helpful, existing studies are based on qualitative themes and to the best of our knowledge, no work has been done on the language features that characterizes helpful support messages.

Language Features for Empathy Empathy is closely related to helpfulness, as many factors contributing to helpfulness (being emotionally warm and compassionate; accepting others' perspectives; practising active listening) are also associated with empathy (Davis, 1983; Baron-Cohen and Wheelwright, 2004; Zhou et al., 2003). There has been significant work on language features that characterize empathy. Sharma et al. (2020) identified that empathy is expressed in language use relating to expressing warm and compassionate emotions, communicating an understanding of others' experience, and asking more about the person's experiences. Xiao et al. (2015) and Gibson et al. (2015) found that language use relating to asking for others' perspective (*e.g.* it sounds like; do you think) are positively associated with empathy while language use that orders other around (*e.g.* you need to; please answer the) are negatively associated with empathy. Language features for empathy overlap with the features that characterize helpfulness, reinforcing the strong connection between empathy and helpfulness.

3 Dataset

Our English dataset is obtained from r/Advice, which allows post authors to mark out comment(s) that they have found helpful[2]. Comments to posts with at least one helpful comment, but were not themselves labeled as helpful are labelled as unhelpful. This inclusion criterion minimizes the mislabelling of comments to posts whose authors did not actively participate in labelling comments. Text from Reddit was downloaded through the Pushshift Application Programming Interface[3]. Suitable posts and all associated comments from the Advice subreddit were downloaded within 300 days (Apr 2019 - Feb 2020). Comments by the post authors and automated bots were excluded. Across the 24964 posts that were downloaded, there were 92477 associated comments (41146 helpful). On average, each comment has 95.8 words (SD=134.5). Training/validation/test split was 80-10-10.

4 How does Helpfulness Relate to Empathy?

To determine how helpfulness relates to empathy, we calculate an aggregated metric for each user based on the proportion of their comments found to be helpful. We then correlate average user helpfulness against an established psychological measure of empathy.

Empathy Quotient Questionnaire The short form of Empathy Quotient (EQ) questionnaire (Wakabayashi et al., 2006) was used to measure empathy (details are in appendix A). Higher scores on the EQ represent higher empathy. The EQ questionnaire has high internal consistency (Cronbach's

[2]This is done using the magic word "helped", which is picked up by AdviceFlairBot

[3]`https://pushshift.io/`

$\alpha = 0.90$) and test-retest reliability after 12 months ($r = 0.97, p < .001$).

Participants Only users with more than 20 comments were included to minimize the likelihood that their average helpfulness was biased due to limited observations. 508 Reddit users were sent an online questionnaire through Reddit and 91 responded. Gender and age were optional to report. 86 participants reported gender (53 male and 33 female) and 83 reported age (M=33.7, SD=13.8). The mean user helpfulness is 0.5440 (SD=0.1956). Using a two-sample t-test, the distribution of EQ scores (M=24.45, SD=8.822, N=91) in this study is found to be not significantly different ($t(1850) = 0.0169, p = 0.9866$) from the sample (M=23.8, SD=8.75, N=1761) in Wakabayashi et al. (2006), demonstrating the representativeness of our sample.

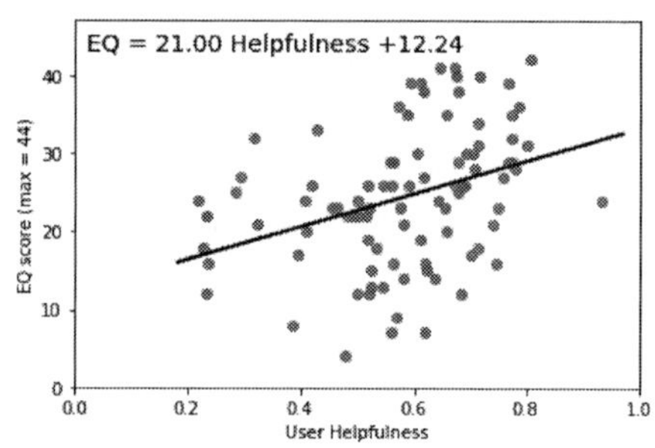

Figure 2: Empathy quotient (EQ) score against User Helpfulness

Results As illustrated in Figure 2, there is a moderate correlation effect between EQ and User helpfulness ($r(91) = 0.359, p < 0.001$). We also explored correlating User helpfulness with various subscales of the EQ, namely cognitive empathy, affective empathy and social skills based on Zhou et al. (2020). Helpfulness correlates most strongly with cognitive empathy ($r(91) = 0.355, p < 0.001$), followed by affective empathy ($r(91) = 0.261, p = 0.012$) and finally social skills ($r(91) = 0.203, p = 0.054$). This suggests that helpful commenters more often are better able to understand how the post authors think compared to how they feel or communicating it across in a social deft manner (which has a boundary p value).

5 Predicting for Helpful Comments

To explore the potential for the dataset to be useful in training models to distinguish between helpful and unhelpful comments, we trained several baseline models and report their micro-average F1 scores. The performance of baseline models on this task is relatively low but similar to the performance on empathy datasets (Gibson et al., 2015; Khanpour et al., 2017; Sharma et al., 2020). The relatively low performance of baseline models on this task suggests that while recognizing helpfulness in language is trivial for typically-developing humans, they remain challenging for machines. Techniques such as commonsense reasoning (Sap et al., 2019; Bosselut et al., 2019) can be explored in the future to better capture the highly complex relationship between language and helpfulness.

	Micro-F1 (σ)
BERT	**69.2 (0.60)**
Logistic Regression	65.4 (0.55)
Naive Bayes	63.0 (0.44)
Support Vector Classifier	63.5 (0.59)
Random Forest	65.1 (0.60)

Table 1: Performance of baseline models on test set. Details of their preparation are in Appendix B

Significant Predictors of Helpfulness To characterize helpfulness in our dataset, significant predictors of helpfulness ($p < 0.05$) based on the Logistic Regression model were extracted and analysed.[4] Thematic categories that were inductively generated from these predictors are shown in Table 4 while word clouds are available in Appendix D.

The first overarching theme is positive and friendly words. Helpfulness is positively predicted by polite, friendly-sounding and optimistic-sounding words but negatively predicted by words that indicate negative emotions. This relates to the literature findings on how uplifting and friendly online support peers are found to be more helpful. (Paulson et al., 1999; Subramani and O'Connor, 2018) Affect-related words (such as sad and tears) were previously found to be significant predictors of empathy (Gibson et al., 2015).

A second overarching theme is words relating to attempts to understand the perspective of others. Helpful commenters do so by addressing post authors directly, instead of patronizing the difficulties that they face. This is also in agreement with

[4]The dataset used to extract the most significant predictors is slightly different. Only one comment was sampled from each post and author to overcome the problem that the covariance matrix was originally non-invertible.

Direction	Themes	Words	Examples
Positive predictors	Polite, friendly sounding words	personally, friend, glad, welcome, feels, hey	Me, **personally**...I'd let it slide. He'd be That's okay I'm just **glad** that you were able to maybe text her? Be like **hey**, just wanted to say
	Optimistic sounding words	good, luck hope, hopefully yes, learned, helped forward, strong,	session with your therapist. **Good luck** **hope** something I say can help you a little! And **yes** that is dangerous and quite work that you can look **forward** to.
	Words addressing the post author directly	you	I really think **you** deserve better. **You** sound like I understand that **you** really like these guys as long as **you** feel **you** are making the best of
Negative predictors	Words indicating negative emotions	victim, kill, rid bad, depression	to be labelled as a **victim**. She might be afraid of I was internalizing every **bad** thing that happened
	Words that patronize the problem faced by the post author	dealt, wish easy, promise advice, told	it's the latter, as I **dealt** with when I was like it seems like the **easy** solution to your situation. The best **advice** I can give you though

Table 2: Thematic categories for significantly predictors of Helpfulness. Statistical analysis in Appendix E

literature on how helpfulness is associated with peers' attempt to accept others' frame of references and experiences. (Subramani and O'Connor, 2018; Green et al., 2020) Furthermore, terms indicating an inclination to find out more about the perspective of others (e.g. "do you think", "it sounds like" and "you think about") were also predictors in empathy datasets (Gibson et al., 2015; Xiao et al., 2015). Overall, the overarching themes that are predictive of helpfulness in our dataset are supported by literature on helpfulness and language features associated with empathy.

6 Human-Annotated Features for Comment Helpfulness

To better understand the capabilities and limitations of language features in capturing comment helpfulness, two graduate students manually annotated a selection of helpful comments. Annotations were done on 5 comments each from 91 authors who responded to our empathy quotient questionnaire. Comments were sampled using a stratified approach that results in a sampled average helpfulness to be closest possible to the author's average helpfulness score ($Pearson's\ r = 0.937, p < 0.001$). Then we labelled each comment with one or more of the 10 possible labels based on helpfulness literature (see Section 2). They are 1. Highly directive, short advice 2. Dismissing concern 3. Negative terms 4. Tangential or unspecific comment 5. Share similar experience 6. Ask clarifying questions 7. Relevant knowledge 8. Emotional support 9. Recognizing difficulty 10. Tentative language. Average Cohen's κ is 0.690 (σ=0.107). Definitions and Cohen's κ for each label are in Appendix 5.

Using a logistic regression, we found that only the use of negative terms and tangential or unspecific comment are negatively associated with helpfulness ($p < 0.05$) while providing relevant knowledge is positively associated ($p < 0.05$). The use of negative terms was also captured by the logistic regression based on language use while the other two factors were not. An inspection of examples revealed that negative terms only comprises of a small set of words while those two factors require contextual semantic understanding of what is relevant knowledge to a situation and what is tangential. Future work can make use of knowledge-enhanced models (Peters et al., 2019; Clark et al., 2021) to better capture such contextual understanding.

7 Conclusion

We introduce and plan to openly release a novel dataset containing helpful and unhelpful comments in response to posts seeking for advice on life issues. We show that the helpfulness of such comments is related to the commenters' empathy and pioneer an analysis into language features predictive of helpful and unhelpful comments on online support communities. Our work can contribute towards supporting people and automated dialogue agents to offer more helpful comments to others.

Ethics and Broader Impact

This project has been approved by University of Cambridge Faculty of Education Institutional Review Board. The use of Reddit data in this project is in alignment with the Reddit End User License Agreement and the Terms of Use for Developers. Because part of the project requires participants to respond to questionnaires, we made sure that the items were phrased sensitively so that no unintended harm would be caused. No payment was made to voluntary participants, as the survey could be done within a few minutes. We also guided participants to make informed decisions about their participation, giving them the opportunity to withdraw any time, during and after the completion of the questionnaire. The collected information, which does not include personally identifiable information, was stored securely with access restricted to the research team. We also manually inspected a small selection of Reddit data to ensure that they do not contain names, personally identifying information or offensive content. We anticipate that this project can accelerate the development of models that can better detect and express helpfulness in social settings, between humans and with social dialogue agents.

References

Simon Baron-Cohen and Sally Wheelwright. 2004. The empathy quotient: An investigation of adults with asperger syndrome or high functioning autism, and normal sex differences. *Journal of Autism and Developmental Disorders*, 34(2):163–175.

Antoine Bosselut, Hannah Rashkin, Maarten Sap, Chaitanya Malaviya, Asli Celikyilmaz, and Yejin Choi. 2019. Comet: Commonsense transformers for automatic knowledge graph construction. In *ACL*.

Katherine Y Chuang and Christopher C Yang. 2012. Interaction patterns of nurturant support exchanged in online health social networking. 14(3):e54.

Thomas Clark, Costanza Conforti, Fangyu Liu, Zaiqiao Meng, Ehsan Shareghi, and Nigel Collier. 2021. Integrating transformers and knowledge graphs for Twitter stance detection. In *Proceedings of the Seventh Workshop on Noisy User-generated Text (W-NUT 2021)*, pages 304–312, Online. Association for Computational Linguistics.

Mark H. Davis. 1983. Measuring individual differences in empathy: Evidence for a multidimensional approach. *Journal of Personality and Social Psychology*, 44(1):113–126.

James Gibson, Nikolaos Malandrakis, Francisco Romero, David Atkins, and Shrikanth S. Narayanan. 2015. Predicting therapist empathy in motivational interviews using language features inspired by psycholinguistic norms. In *Proceedings of Interspeech*.

Brian M Green, Katelyn Tente Van Horn, Ketki Gupte, Megan Evans, Sara Hayes, and Amrita Bhowmick. 2020. Assessment of adaptive engagement and support model for people with chronic health conditions in online health communities: Combined content analysis. 22(7):e17338.

David M. Greenberg, Varun Warrier, Carrie Allison, and Simon Baron-Cohen. 2018. Testing the empathizing–systemizing theory of sex differences and the extreme male brain theory of autism in half a million people. *Proceedings of the National Academy of Sciences*, 115(48):12152–12157.

Y. Groen, A. B. M. Fuermaier, A. E. Den Heijer, O. Tucha, and M. Althaus. 2015. The empathy and systemizing quotient: The psychometric properties of the dutch version and a review of the cross-cultural stability. *Journal of Autism and Developmental Disorders*, 45(9):2848–2864.

Hamed Khanpour, Cornelia Caragea, and Prakhar Biyani. 2017. Identifying empathetic messages in online health communities. In *Proceedings of the Eighth International Joint Conference on Natural Language Processing (Volume 2: Short Papers)*, pages 246–251, Taipei, Taiwan. Asian Federation of Natural Language Processing.

Vladimir Kosonogov. 2014. The psychometric properties of the russian version of the empathy quotient. *Psychology in Russia: State of the Art*, 7:96–104.

Aidan McKiernan, Patrick Ryan, Eimear McMahon, Stephen Bradley, and Ellen Butler. 2018. Understanding young people's relationship breakups using the dual processing model of coping and bereavement. 23(3):192–210.

Barbara L. Paulson, Derek Truscott, and Janice Stuart. 1999. Clients' perceptions of helpful experiences in counseling. 46(3):317–324.

Trena M. Paulus and Mary Alice Varga. 2015. "please know that you are not alone with your pain": Responses to newcomer posts in an online grief support forum. 39(10):633–640.

Matthew E. Peters, Mark Neumann, Robert Logan, Roy Schwartz, Vidur Joshi, Sameer Singh, and Noah A. Smith. 2019. Knowledge enhanced contextual word representations. In *Proceedings of the 2019 Conference on Empirical Methods in Natural Language Processing and the 9th International Joint Conference on Natural Language Processing (EMNLP-IJCNLP)*, pages 43–54, Hong Kong, China. Association for Computational Linguistics.

Maarten Sap, Ronan Le Bras, Emily Allaway, Chandra Bhagavatula, Nicholas Lourie, Hannah Rashkin, Brendan Roof, Noah A. Smith, and Yejin Choi. 2019. Atomic: An atlas of machine commonsense for if-then reasoning. *Proceedings of the AAAI Conference on Artificial Intelligence*, 33(01):3027–3035.

Marijke Schotanus-Dijkstra, Petra Havinga, Wouter van Ballegooijen, Lynn Delfosse, Jan Mokkenstorm, and Brigitte Boon. 2014. What do the bereaved by suicide communicate in online support groups? 35(1):27–35.

Ashish Sharma, Adam Miner, David Atkins, and Tim Althoff. 2020. A computational approach to understanding empathy expressed in text-based mental health support. In *Proceedings of the 2020 Conference on Empirical Methods in Natural Language Processing (EMNLP)*, pages 5263–5276, Online. Association for Computational Linguistics.

Sudha Subramani and Manjula O'Connor. 2018. Extracting actionable knowledge from domestic violence discourses on social media. 5(17):154807.

Akio Wakabayashi, Simon Baron-Cohen, Sally Wheelwright, Nigel Goldenfeld, Joe Delaney, Debra Fine, Richard Smith, and Leonora Weil. 2006. Development of short forms of the empathy quotient (EQ-short) and the systemizing quotient (SQ-short). *Personality and Individual Differences*, 41(5):929–940.

Bo Xiao, Zac E. Imel, Panayiotis G. Georgiou, David C. Atkins, and Shrikanth S. Narayanan. 2015. "rate my therapist": Automated detection of empathy in drug and alcohol counseling via speech and language processing. *PLOS ONE*, 10(12):1–15.

Ningning Zhou, Danni Wang, Gregory S. Chasson, Xin Xu, Jianping Wang, and Maria Izabel Lockwood. 2020. Psychometric properties of the chinese empathy and systemizing quotients in a non-clinical sample.

Qing Zhou, Carlos Valiente, and Nancy Eisenberg. 2003. Empathy and its measurement. *Positive psychological assessment: A handbook of models and measures.*, page 269–284.

A Empathy Quotient Questionnaire

Items originate from the long form of Empathy Quotient questionnaire (Baron-Cohen and Wheelwright, 2004), which is well-cited (>3500 citations) and demonstrates good validity in large (>500,000) and culturally-diverse samples (Kosonogov, 2014; Groen et al., 2015; Greenberg et al., 2018). The short form was chosen to reduce the time taken to answer the questionnaire and thereby increase the response rate. The short form is a 22-item forced-choice self-report questionnaire that can be answered on a four-point Likert Scale (Strongly Agree, Agree, Disagree, Strongly Disagree). Questions include "I often find it difficult to judge if something is rude or polite", "I can pick up quickly if someone says one thing but means another", and "I am good at predicting how someone will feel". Each response can give 0, 1 or 2 points, leading to a maximum total EQ score of 44.

B Baseline Models

Each model was run with 5 different random seeds.

BERT Pre-trained BERT English-base-uncased WordPiece tokenizer was used. We fine-tuned a BERT Sequence Prediction model (English-base-uncased version with 12-layer, 768-hidden, 12-heads, 110M parameters accessed from `https://github.com/huggingface/transformers`). BertAdam optimizer was used with 0.1 epoch for warmup and learning rate of $2 * 10^{-6}$ following a search within $\{1,2,5\} * 10^n$, $-6 \geq n \geq -4$ using F1 as criterion. Maximum sequence length was 512 tokens, batch-size was 8 and epoch number was 2. Training took 4 hours on a Nvidia P100 GPU.

Others Text was split up into individual words and lower-cased. The number of times each word occurred in each text was then counted. Words that occurred fewer than ten times altogether were removed to minimize the effects of misspelled or rare words. Logistic Regression, Linear Support Vector Classifier, Multinomial Naive Bayes and Random Forest models were trained (accessed from `https://scikit-learn.org/stable/`) All hyperparameters were default except adjusting the number of estimators in the Random Forest model to 100. Training took negligible time (< 0.5 hours) on CPU.

C Performance of Baseline Models (Validation Set)

	Micro-F1 (σ)
BERT	**69.5 (0.52)**
Logistic Regression	65.1 (0.12)
Naive Bayes	62.9 (0.40)
Support Vector Classifier	63.5 (0.34)
Random Forest	65.2 (0.33)

Table 3: Performance of baseline models on validation set.

D Word Clouds of Significant Predictors of Helpfulness

Size of words are directly proportional to their significance of correlation.

Figure 3: Significant positive predictors of helpfulness

Figure 4: Significant negative predictors o helpfulness

E Statistical Description for Each Theme

F Labels and Descriptions for Manual Annotation of Helpfulness

G Empathy Questionnaire Instructions

Direction	Themes	Words	Mean Info. Gain	Proportion (%)		
				Total	Helpful	Unhelpful
Positive predictors	Polite, friendly sounding words	personally, friend, glad, welcome, feels, hey	0.002759	11.7	16.1	8.14
	Optimistic sounding words	good, luck hope, hopefully yes, learned, helped forward, strong,	0.00431	27.6	37.0	20.0
	Words addressing the post author directly	you	0.0484	73.2	84.4	64.2
Negative predictors	Words indicating negative emotions	victim, kill, rid bad, depression	0.000712	7.81	9.67	6.32
	Words that patronize the problem faced by the post author	dealt, wish easy, promise advice, told	0.000864	12.2	15.3	9.67

Table 4: Statistical Description for themes identified from significantly predictors of Helpfulness. Helpful comments contain more words from both positive and negative predictors, but the gap between helpful and unhelpful comments is greater for positive predictors.

Label	Description	Cohen's κ
Highly directive, short advice	Extremely short advice that are directing what the post author should do (commonly yes, no, go do this! etc)	0.724
Dismissing concern	Saying that what the post author is going through is not a big deal	0.662
Negative terms	Mentioning negative terms that the author did not bring up (crazy, psycho etc).	0.788
Tangential or unspecific comment	Mentioning random terms that has nothing to do with the author's post.	0.794
Share similar experience	Bringing up that the comment author experienced something similar as the post author	0.677
Ask clarifying questions	Asking questions to clarify what the author's situation really is. Alternatively, they can be saying "If it's situation A then . . . , otherwise if situation B then . . . "	0.644
Relevant knowledge	Bringing any knowledge to help solve the post author's specific situation (for instance, something like "you can try . . . " or "there is this resource . . . ")	0.802
Emotional support	Offering emotional comfort to the post author (something like I am sure this will get better or It's definitely not your fault)	0.650
Recognizing difficulty	Acknowledging that it's a very bad situation for the author to be in (I'm sorry that this is a really bad situation)	0.419*
Tentative language	Phrasing advice as tentative suggestions – such as using "you might want to try . . . " or " I am no expert on this but . . . "	0.739

Table 5: Labels, descriptions and Cohen's κ for manual annotation of helpfulness in comments. * Cohen's κ for "Recognizing difficulty" is low due to the very low number of positive labels (<5%)

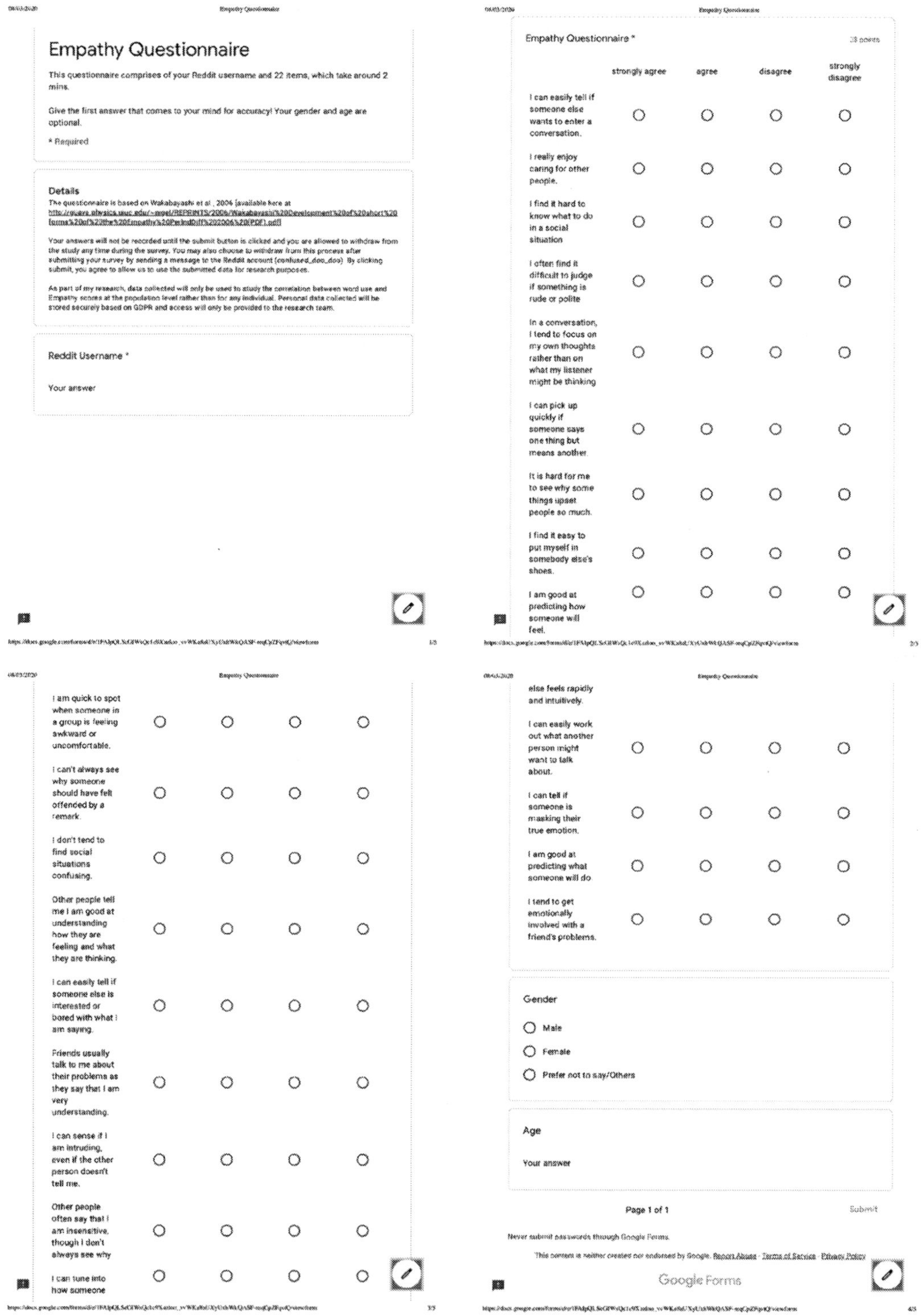

Empathy Questionnaire

This questionnaire comprises of your Reddit username and 22 items, which take around 2 mins.

Give the first answer that comes to your mind for accuracy! Your gender and age are optional.

* Required

Details

The questionnaire is based on Wakabayashi et al., 2006 [available here at http://guava.physics.uiuc.edu/~nigel/REPRINTS/2006/Wakabayashi%20Development%20of%20short%20forms%20of%20the%20Empathy%20Pw...%202006%20(PDF).pdf]

Your answers will not be recorded until the submit button is clicked and you are allowed to withdraw from the study any time during the survey. You may also choose to withdraw from this process after submitting your survey by sending a message to the Reddit account (confused_doo_doo). By clicking submit, you agree to allow us to use the submitted data for research purposes.

As part of my research, data collected will only be used to study the correlation between word use and Empathy scores at the population level rather than for any individual. Personal data collected will be stored securely based on GDPR and access will only be provided to the research team.

Reddit Username *

Your answer

Empathy Questionnaire * 22 points

	strongly agree	agree	disagree	strongly disagree
I can easily tell if someone else wants to enter a conversation.	○	○	○	○
I really enjoy caring for other people.	○	○	○	○
I find it hard to know what to do in a social situation	○	○	○	○
I often find it difficult to judge if something is rude or polite	○	○	○	○
In a conversation, I tend to focus on my own thoughts rather than on what my listener might be thinking	○	○	○	○
I can pick up quickly if someone says one thing but means another	○	○	○	○
It is hard for me to see why some things upset people so much.	○	○	○	○
I find it easy to put myself in somebody else's shoes.	○	○	○	○
I am good at predicting how someone will feel.	○	○	○	○
I am quick to spot when someone in a group is feeling awkward or uncomfortable.	○	○	○	○
I can't always see why someone should have felt offended by a remark.	○	○	○	○
I don't tend to find social situations confusing.	○	○	○	○
Other people tell me I am good at understanding how they are feeling and what they are thinking.	○	○	○	○
I can easily tell if someone else is interested or bored with what I am saying.	○	○	○	○
Friends usually talk to me about their problems as they say that I am very understanding.	○	○	○	○
I can sense if I am intruding, even if the other person doesn't tell me.	○	○	○	○
Other people often say that I am insensitive, though I don't always see why	○	○	○	○
I can tune into how someone else feels rapidly and intuitively.	○	○	○	○
I can easily work out what another person might want to talk about.	○	○	○	○
I can tell if someone is masking their true emotion.	○	○	○	○
I am good at predicting what someone will do	○	○	○	○
I tend to get emotionally involved with a friend's problems.	○	○	○	○

Gender

○ Male

○ Female

○ Prefer not to say/Others

Age

Your answer

Page 1 of 1 Submit

Never submit passwords through Google Forms.

This content is neither created nor endorsed by Google. Report Abuse · Terms of Service · Privacy Policy

Google Forms

Figure 5: Empathy questionnaire instructions

GPT-2-based Human-in-the-loop Theatre Play Script Generation*

Rudolf Rosa,$^{\mu}$ **Patrícia Schmidtová,**$^{\mu}$ **Ondřej Dušek,**$^{\mu}$ **Tomáš Musil,**$^{\mu}$ **David Mareček,**$^{\mu}$ **Saad Obaid,**$^{\mu}$ **Marie Nováková,**$^{\sigma\mu}$ **Klára Vosecká**$^{\delta}$ and **Josef Doležal**$^{\delta}$
$^{\mu}$Charles University, Faculty of Mathematics and Physics, Prague, Czechia
$^{\sigma}$The Švanda Theatre in Smíchov, Prague, Czechia
$^{\delta}$The Academy of Performing Arts in Prague, Theatre Faculty (DAMU), Prague, Czechia
rosa@ufal.mff.cuni.cz

Abstract

We experiment with adapting generative language models for the generation of long coherent narratives in the form of theatre plays. Since fully automatic generation of whole plays is not currently feasible, we created an interactive tool that allows a human user to steer the generation somewhat while minimizing intervention. We pursue two approaches to long-text generation: a flat generation with summarization of context, and a hierarchical text-to-text two-stage approach, where a synopsis is generated first and then used to condition generation of the final script. Our preliminary results and discussions with theatre professionals show improvements over vanilla language model generation, but also identify important limitations of our approach.

1 Introduction

Natural language generation (NLG) is currently dominated by large pre-trained language models, such as GPT-3 (Brown et al., 2020). The models show especially strong performance in generating short to medium length in-domain texts, such as news stories, which fit into the window size of the model (e.g. 512 or 1,024 subword tokens). Successfully handling significantly larger and/or out-of-domain documents is a matter of ongoing research (Beltagy et al., 2020; Zaheer et al., 2020; Gururangan et al., 2020; Chen et al., 2020).

In the THEaiTRE project, we focus on generating theatre play scripts. This task combines the challenges of narrative generation (Riedl, 2016) and dialogue generation (Wen et al., 2016), and could be seen either as generating dialogues with a very large context, or as generating a narrative in the form of a dialogue. Additional challenges include the complex structure of the theatre scripts (including setting descriptions, dialogue lines with character names, and stage directions), their very large length, their pseudo-multi-author nature (as lines pertaining to different characters use different styles and represent different standpoints), or the low availability of large in-domain datasets.

We investigate the capabilities of current NLG approaches on this task. Specifically, we use and adapt current large pre-trained neural language models and employ other relevant natural language processing (NLP) techniques to adjust the existing approaches and tools to the theatrical script domain.

Our aim is to produce a mostly automatically generated play, with minimal human-in-the-loop interventions, and have the generated play rehearsed and staged by a theatre. We build upon our previous work (Rosa et al., 2021), where we produced a generated play by using vanilla GPT-2 and generated individual, loosely connected scenes, but now aim at full play generation. In order to do so, we explore a two-phase hierarchical text-to-text approach, where a synopsis is generated first and then used as a basis for subsequent generation of scenes. We compare this method to a flat generation approach with summarization, which is similar to our previous work (Rosa et al., 2021). We use models finetuned on in-domain theatre or movie scripts to better fit the domain, and we allow minimal but precise human intervention using a custom-built web-based interface: regenerating a line, choosing the next character to speak, deleting or inserting a generated or a human-written line into the script. All human interventions are recorded. A simplified demo version of the tool used for the generation is freely available online.[1] We include preliminary intrinsic evaluation and discuss qualitative feedback given by the theatre professionals. Our results support finetuning and more precise human intervention; however, the two-stage hierarchical approach shows difficulties following the pre-generated synopsis.

*Archival WNU submission.

[1]https://theaitre.com/demo

Proceedings of the 3rd Wordplay: When Language Meets Games Workshop (Wordplay 2022), pages 29 - 37
July 15, 2022

2 Related Work

Our approach is inspired by the work of Fan et al. (2018) and Fan et al. (2019), who propose a hierarchical system for story generation. A similar idea has been explored by Rashkin et al. (2020), who generate a story conditioned on a given outline. Tan et al. (2021) approach long text generation by generating domain-specific words first and then iteratively refining it until whole sentences are formed. Unlike these works, we generate scripts rather than stories, i.e. not prose but dialogues, which are also longer than typical stories. For dialogue generation, Xu et al. (2021)'s work is close to our baseline flat approach (Section 3) in that they generate long dialogues by using summarization.

A few works also investigate human-machine interaction during text generation, with different aims from ours: Roemmele (2021) investigates how automatically generated texts can inspire human writing. Akoury et al. (2020) use the amount of required human post-editing as a story quality metric.

A number of language generation tools is available online, both free and paid, typically based on GPT-2 and GPT-3 language models (Radford et al., 2019; Brown et al., 2020), sometimes trained or fine-tuned for a specific domain or task. Prominent examples include news generators such as *Grover*[2] by Zellers et al. (2019) or *News You Can't Use*[3] by Geitgey (2019), the text adventure game *AI Dungeon*,[4] the code completion tools *GitHub Copilot*[5] or *Deep Tabnine*,[6] and chatbots such as *AI|Writer* or *Project December*.[7] However, to the best of our knowledge, no generation tool has been released specifically for theatre scripts.

There have been several other projects using automatically generated scripts, including *Beyond the Fence*, a musical based on suggestions from several automated tools (Colton et al., 2016), *Sunspring*, a short sci-fi movie with an LSTM-generated script (Benjamin et al., 2016), *Lifestyle of the Richard and Family*, a theatre play written with the help of a next word suggestion tool (Helper, 2018), or the performances of the *Improbotics* group who improvise on stage with real-time GPT-3-generated lines (Mathewson and Mirowski, 2017). However, the tools used in these projects are not publicly available online, and often there is little transparency about the particularities of the exact design and usage of the tools. Moreover, these projects typically use substantial human curation.

[2] https://rowanzellers.com/grover/
[3] https://newsyoucantuse.com/
[4] https://play.aidungeon.io/
[5] https://copilot.github.com/
[6] https://www.tabnine.com/
[7] https://projectdecember.net/

Domain	# Scripts	Avg. # Lines	Avg. # Sentences
Movies	1,067	783	2,537
TV Shows	6,057	314	902
Theatre	5,517	530	1,529
All	12,641	446	1,310

Table 1: A brief overview of the script dataset we use for finetuning.

3 Flat Generation with Summarization

The flat generation variant is based on our previous approach (Rosa et al., 2021) of using a standard generative model but employing extractive text summarization to deal with the limited window (1,024 tokens for GPT-2) so that longer scripts can be generated without the loss of the global context. Instead of using a vanilla GPT-2 model as in our previous work, we finetune our models on a large collection of ca. 12k theatre and movie scripts. The domains and volumes of data can be found in Table 1. The theatre plays and TV shows scripts were scraped from various websites, the movie section comes from (Lison and Meena, 2016).

The operation of flat generation looks as follows: the user inputs a scene setting, character names and their first lines, from which we construct the input prompt in the following format:

```
Scene setting.

Character Name: Character line.

Character Name: Character line.
```

The model then generates a continuation of the script line by line (see Figure 2).[8] At each step, the user can choose whether they want to regenerate the last generated line (i.e. generate a different continuation), or whether they want to continue by generating a further line. They can also choose the next character and let the model generate their line, or insert/delete lines within the generated text. A screenshot of this tool is presented in Figure 1.

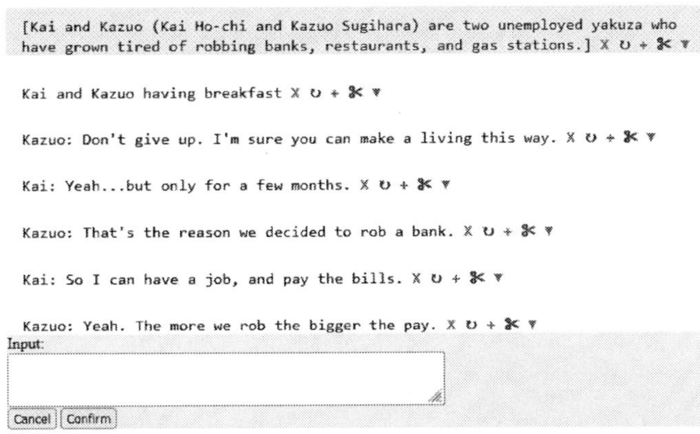

Figure 1: A screenshot of the tool used for the generation. The cross generates an alternative continuation starting with the given line. The arrow creates an alternative line while keeping the script continuation. The plus symbol generates and inserts a line, while the scissors symbol deletes it without any changes to the continuation in both cases. Finally, the triangle symbol allows for human input that prompts the regeneration of the continuation.

Polonius speaks to the king. Enter Hamlet.	
Polonius:	I hear him coming; let's hide, sir.
Hamlet:	To be or not to be; that is the question.
Polonius:	That is the reason, Hamlet. You are a good man.
Hamlet:	I am but what I am.
Polonius:	You are a bad man.

Figure 2: Flat script generation example. The initial human-written prompt is shown above the dividing line, the following generated outputs follow below.

A notebook full of ideas was stolen from an unbuttoned backpack by a mailman in a blue vest.
A man named Tom, a man in a trench coat, arrives to deliver the notebook.
Tom tries to leave, but is interrupted by the arrival of his mailman brother, Jerry, in his mail truck.
Jerry offers to take Tom to his house, but Tom is determined to deliver the notebook. As Tom drives through the cornfield, he accidentally stops at a house, which he mistakenly assumes is inhabited by the owner, a widowed woman named Marjorie.
She tells him she is waiting for Tom to come home, and she and Tom go into the house together.
Jerry arrives and finds Tom's truck with the notebook, having accidentally left it in the truck while searching for Jerry, and is surprised and angry to find Marjorie there.

Figure 3: An example for hierarchical generation 1st phase: title to synopsis (input title shown above the dividing line, the play follows below).

4 Two-phase Hierarchical Generation

Our second, newly developed approach is a two-phase text-to-text hierarchical generation approach: (1) a synopsis is generated from a user-supplied play title, (2) the play dialogue is generated, conditioned on the title and a part of the synopsis. Both phases use specific models finetuned on our in-domain datasets.

The input for the first phase is the title of the play, from which the synopsis of the play is generated (Figure 3, Section 4.1). At each step, The user has the option of continuing generation, regenerating or deleting lines (roughly corresponding to sentences). Once the user is satisfied with the generated synopsis (or the generation ends by the model generating the *endoftext* token), the synopsis is used as input for the second phase.

In the second phase, shown in Figure 4, the play script is generated from the synopsis (see Section 4.2). The user is now provided with a set of options similar to the flat approach: at each step choosing between generating a character line (and potentially also choosing which character should speak the line) or moving on to the next part of the generated synopsis.

4.1 1st Phase: Synopsis generation

The goal of this phase is to generate a synopsis based on a user-specified play title. For this, we finetune pretrained language models on a dataset consisting of synopses of theatre plays (scraped by us from Wikipedia), movies (Robischon, 2018; Kar et al., 2018), TV series (scraped by us from various fan wiki pages) and books (Bamman and

[8]The GPT-2 model sticks to the input format and generates a dialogue-like output; this is mostly true even for vanilla models, let alone a model finetuned specifically for this task.

Model	Avg. # Sentences	Avg. # Words	Vocab Size	Entropy
Vanilla GPT-2	38.10	285.80	1,371	1.72
Finetuned GPT-2	29.32	536.74	1,995	3.48
Finetuned PEGASUS	14.80	281.40	1,416	2.65
Finetuned DistilBART	27.00	526.33	1,182	2.43

Table 2: Basic characteristics of synopsis generation model outputs (average output lengths in terms of sentences and words, total number of distinct words used on the output, Shannon entropy over all outputs).

Model	Coherence	Consistency	Originality	Relevance	Overall Impression
Vanilla GPT-2	2.7	2.8	2.6	**2.7**	2.6
Finetuned GPT-2	**3.0**	**3.1**	3.1	2.6	**3.2**
Finetuned PEGASUS	2.8	2.8	3.0	2.1	2.8
Finetuned DistilBART	1.9	2.0	**3.2**	2.0	2.9

Table 3: Results of human evaluation of synopsis generation models (1 to 5 points, higher is better). The presented values are the average values across the annotator scores.

A notebook full of ideas was stolen from an unbuttoned backpack by a mailman in a blue vest.
A man named Tom, a man in a trench coat, arrives to deliver the notebook.

Tom:	We've got an urgent message to deliver to your office.
Man:	That's impossible! Why'd you bring me here if you were planning to rob the post office?

Figure 4: An example for hierarchical generation 2nd phase: synopsis to script. The script generated in the bottom section is conditioned on the human-written prompt and a line from the generated synopsis, shown in the top section. The user has the option to continue generating automatically, or to control the next character speaking (choose from the previously used ones or input manually).

Smith, 2017). The final dataset contains over 50k title-synopsis pairs.

We finetuned three different models on our dataset for 15 epochs – GPT2-medium, Pegasus (Zhang et al., 2019), and DistilBART (Shleifer and Rush, 2020). Some basic statistics of all the models are shown in Table 2, comparing to a vanilla GPT2 baseline. We can see that all models show similar scores. To choose the best synopsis model, we performed a small-scale human evaluation with 6 lay annotators rating 12 synopses generated by each model.

The annotators were shown one story at a time and were asked to answer the following questions using a 1 (worst) to 5 (best) Likert scale rating:

1. Is the text **coherent**?
2. Are the characters **consistent**?
3. Is the text **original** and/or interesting?
4. Is the title **relevant** to the story?
5. How much did you **enjoy** reading this text?

Based on the results of this evaluation (Table 3), we picked out GPT2-medium[9] as the best one due to its highest overall impression score (Question 5) and strong performance in the remaining evaluated aspects.

4.2 2nd Phase: Script generation

In the second phase, we generate the play script from a pre-generated synopsis. As operating on the whole potentially very long synopsis, let alone the whole script, is beyond the capabilities of current models, we split the synopsis into smaller chunks, and consecutively take each of the chunks as input for generating a part of the script.[10]

Data preparation and alignment

A major challenge is obtaining the training dataset. Ideally, we would use a set of theatre scripts and corresponding synopses. However, due to licensing and copyright issues, such data are not available to us, except for a modest number of mostly very old plays. Therefore, we use a near-domain ScriptBase corpus (Gorinski and Lapata, 2018), which contains movie scripts and their synopses.[11]

Both synopses and scripts in ScriptBase are split

[9]Trained with a $1e^{-5}$ learning rate with warm up.

[10]This is motivated by the notion of a theatre script being split into individual scenes, which are partially independent. However, we do not guarantee that our chunks actually correspond to individual scenes, as we have not trained a scene splitter for synopses; therefore, we simply split the synopsis into individual sentences with a sentence splitter.

[11]Another option could be GraphMovie (Zhu et al., 2020), a similar dataset with better annotations but only available in Chinese.

Algorithm 1 Scene alignment.

Input: $\{c_i\}_1^N$ ▷ Script SBERT embeddings
Input: $\{m_j\}_1^M$ ▷ Synopsis SBERT embeddings
  $s_{1,j} \leftarrow cos(c_1, m_j)$ ▷ Forward pass
  for $i \in \{2, \ldots, N\}, j \in \{1, \ldots, M\}$ **do**
    $s_{i,j} \leftarrow cos(c_j, m_j) + max\{s_{i-1,j-1}, s_{i-1,j}\}$
  end for
  $a_N \leftarrow M$ ▷ Backward pass
  for $i \in \{N, \ldots, 2\}$ **do**
    $a_{i-1} \leftarrow \arg\max_{j \in \{a_i - 1, a_i\}} s_{i-1,j}$
  end for
  return $\{a_i\}_1^N$ ▷ Each c_i aligned to m_{a_i}

into scenes, but the granularity is different. The scripts are divided into many very short scenes, sometimes consisting of only one utterance or scenic remark, and a scene synopsis often corresponds to tens of script scenes. We thus use the synopsis scenes, and align script scenes to them in a many-to-one fashion. The resulting dataset contains pairs of synopsis scenes and their aligned script scenes.

First, we process the scripts by removing short one-line scenes or merging them with adjacent scenes: If the line is uttered by a character also present in the previous scene (preferably) or the subsequent scene, we merge the two scenes. Otherwise, we remove the scene; this includes scenes consisting only of a scenic remark.[12]

We then represent each script scene i and each synopsis scene j with its SBERT embeddings (Reimers and Gurevych, 2019) c_i or m_j, and align each script scene to the synopsis scene a_i using dynamic programming with Algorithm 1. In the forward pass, the algorithm computes a scene pair alignment score $s_{i,j}$ as the cosine similarity of the embeddings, plus the score of the best candidate alignment for aligning the preceding script scene $(i-1)$ to either the same synopsis scene (j) or to the preceding synopsis scene $(j-1)$. The final alignment is computed in the backward pass, assuming the alignment of the last scenes to each other, and iteratively taking the best candidate alignment (a_i or $a_i - 1$) for the preceding script scene $(i-1)$.

Furthermore, we filter the alignments by a threshold on SBERT cosine similarity of 0.3 (determined empirically). We thus create two versions of training data for the script generation models (see Table 4 for details).

[12]According to our cursory checks, this does not have a dramatic impact on overall coherence, as such scenes are usually not logically connected.

Variant	# Scenes	Script-synopsis ratio	Avg. # lines
Base	14,655	3.40	54.98
Filtered	11,957	3.70	60.97

Table 4: Statistics of aligned synopsis-script scenes used for hierarchical generation (script-synopsis ratio is the average number of script scenes aligned to a single synopsis scene).

Script generation model

We use the GPT2-medium model finetuned for flat script generation (see Section 3) and finetune it further for the task of generating a script chunk from a synopsis chunk, using both dataset variants created in the previous subsection. For each synopsis scene as the input prompt, we train the model to generate the corresponding script scene. The model uses a $1e^{-5}$ learning rate for 10 epochs with warm up.

A basic comparison using intrinsic statistics (scripts generated based on 6 identical prompts) is shown in Table 5. While the scripts generated by the Hierarchical variant are shorter on average, they tend to be more variable, using a more varied vocabulary and showing higher entropy and perplexity, which points at less repetitiveness.

5 Discussion and Limitations

Generating theatre play scripts is a complex task presenting many interesting challenges, many of which we have not yet been able to satisfactorily address, as we are continually being informed by theatre professionals.

The main weakness of all our approaches is the inability to differentiate between individual characters to ensure their lines are cohesive while being distinct from other characters in the play. The theatre professionals consider it difficult to portray characters missing a consistent personality and motives behind the lines. While our past as well as ongoing experiments, employing natural language inference, line masking, and character pseudonymization, have shown promising results, they only seem to constitute partial superficial remedies for a deep and complex issue. In the future, we intend to approach the problem by adapting and employing current NLG personalization techniques (Yang and Flek, 2021).

Model	Avg. # Lines	Avg. # Sentences	Avg. # Words	Vocab Size	Entropy	Perplexity
Vanilla GPT-2	7.33	203.00	500.83	863	2.71	5.19
Finetuned GPT-2: Flat	5.67	94.33	724.50	981	3.09	6.30
Finetuned GPT-2: Hier./Base	5.00	68.00	769.50	1,336	2.93	9.77
Finetuned GPT-2: Hier./Filtered	5.67	61.50	678.00	1,335	2.72	21.87

Table 5: A basic statistics comparison for script generation by different model variants. Cf. Table 2 for metrics details; perplexity is measured using vanilla GPT2-XL.

Another serious problem, identified by the theatre professionals while working with our hierarchical setup, is the fact that the script generation often strays away from the synopsis. So far, we have been only operating with flat textual representations of script parts in the hierarchical setup, aligning parts of the script to parts of its synopsis. While we believe the currently available data leave us no other option, a more adequate approach should probably operate with theatrological abstractions over the script, such as the notion of dramatic situations of Polti (1921); we have performed some small-scale annotations of 50 play scripts in this respect, but our exploratory experiments on the resulting dataset showed that we would require a much larger dataset to be able to employ current machine learning techniques, which is beyond our budget. Unfortunately, corpora of theatrical texts, even unannotated ones, are virtually non-existent, and while we managed to acquire a modest dataset, copyright and licensing issues limit us from releasing most of it.

The use of extractive summarization and hierarchical generation allows us to generate medium-length texts (one or several scenes), but a full-length script is still somewhat out of our reach. We believe further improvements could be brought by employing *abstractive* summarization (Paulus et al., 2018), specifically trained for theatre play scripts.

6 Conclusion

We created an interactive tool for human-in-the-loop generation of theatre play scripts, with the aim of producing a stageable play with minimal human intervention. We pursue two different approaches, both based on finetuned GPT-2 models – flat generation with extractive summarization to maintain coherence, and a hierarchical two-stage approach, which first generates a textual synopsis and then generates individual scenes, conditioning on chunks of the synopsis. We release an online demo of our tool for interactive generation of theatre play scripts. We are able to improve upon previous approaches using vanilla models, but our models still are not able to generate consistent personality or follow the synopsis accurately without human intervention.

A demo of our interactive tool and its source codes are available online.[13] In future work, we plan to incorporate natural language inference checks (Welleck et al., 2019) or experiment with dialogue act semantic representations (Kumar et al., 2018) in order to increase coherence. To improve character consistency, we plan to follow per-character personalization approaches (Yang and Flek, 2021).

Acknowledgements

The project *TL03000348 THEaiTRE: Umělá inteligence autorem divadelní hry* is co-financed with the state support of Technological Agency of the Czech Republic within the ETA 3 Programme. The work described herein has been using data, tools and services provided by the LINDAT/CLARIAH-CZ Research Infrastructure (https://lindat.cz), supported by the Ministry of Education, Youth and Sports of the Czech Republic (Project No. LM2018101).

References

Nader Akoury, Shufan Wang, Josh Whiting, Stephen Hood, Nanyun Peng, and Mohit Iyyer. 2020. STORIUM: A Dataset and Evaluation Platform for Machine-in-the-Loop Story Generation. In *Proceedings of the 2020 Conference on Empirical Methods in Natural Language Processing (EMNLP)*, pages 6470–6484, Online. Association for Computational Linguistics.

David Bamman and Noah Smith. 2017. Cmu book summary dataset.

Iz Beltagy, Matthew E Peters, and Arman Cohan. 2020. Longformer: The long-document transformer. *arXiv preprint arXiv:2004.05150*.

[13]Demo: `https://theaitre.com/demo`, sources: `https://github.com/ufal/theaitrobot`

AI Benjamin, Oscar Sharp, and Ross Goodwin. 2016. Sunspring, a sci-fi short film starring Thomas Middleditch.

Tom B Brown, Benjamin Mann, Nick Ryder, Melanie Subbiah, Jared Kaplan, Prafulla Dhariwal, Arvind Neelakantan, Pranav Shyam, Girish Sastry, Amanda Askell, et al. 2020. Language models are few-shot learners. *arXiv preprint arXiv:2005.14165*.

Zhiyu Chen, Harini Eavani, Wenhu Chen, Yinyin Liu, and William Yang Wang. 2020. Few-shot NLG with pre-trained language model. In *Proceedings of the 58th Annual Meeting of the Association for Computational Linguistics*, pages 183–190, Online. Association for Computational Linguistics.

Simon Colton, Maria Teresa Llano, Rose Hepworth, John Charnley, Catherine V. Gale, Archie Baron, François Pachet, Pierre Roy, Pablo Gervás, Nick Collins, Bob Sturm, Tillman Weyde, Daniel Wolff, and James Robert Lloyd. 2016. The Beyond the Fence musical and Computer Says Show documentary. In *Proceedings of the Seventh International Conference on Computational Creativity*.

Angela Fan, Mike Lewis, and Yann Dauphin. 2018. Hierarchical neural story generation. In *Proceedings of the 56th Annual Meeting of the Association for Computational Linguistics (Volume 1: Long Papers)*, pages 889–898, Melbourne, Australia. Association for Computational Linguistics.

Angela Fan, Mike Lewis, and Yann Dauphin. 2019. Strategies for structuring story generation. In *Proceedings of the 57th Annual Meeting of the Association for Computational Linguistics*, pages 2650–2660, Florence, Italy. Association for Computational Linguistics.

Adam Geitgey. 2019. *Machine Learning is Fun!* Self-published.

Philip John Gorinski and Mirella Lapata. 2018. What's this movie about? A joint neural network architecture for movie content analysis. In *Proceedings of NAACL-HLT*, pages 1770–1781, New Orleans, Louisiana.

Suchin Gururangan, Ana Marasović, Swabha Swayamdipta, Kyle Lo, Iz Beltagy, Doug Downey, and Noah A. Smith. 2020. Don't stop pretraining: Adapt language models to domains and tasks. In *Proceedings of the 58th Annual Meeting of the Association for Computational Linguistics*, pages 8342–8360, Online. Association for Computational Linguistics.

Roslyn Helper. 2018. Lifestyle of the Richard and family.

Sudipta Kar, Suraj Maharjan, A. Pastor López-Monroy, and Thamar Solorio. 2018. MPST: A corpus of movie plot synopses with tags. In *Proceedings of the Eleventh International Conference on Language Resources and Evaluation (LREC 2018)*, Paris, France. European Language Resources Association (ELRA).

Harshit Kumar, Arvind Agarwal, and Sachindra Joshi. 2018. Dialogue-act-driven Conversation Model : An Experimental Study. In *Proceedings of the 27th International Conference on Computational Linguistics*, pages 1246–1256, Santa Fe, New Mexico, USA. Association for Computational Linguistics.

Pierre Lison and Raveesh Meena. 2016. Automatic Turn Segmentation for Movie & TV Subtitles. In *2016 IEEE Workshop on Spoken Language Technology*. IEEE conference proceedings.

Kory W Mathewson and Piotr Mirowski. 2017. Improvised theatre alongside artificial intelligences. In *Thirteenth Artificial Intelligence and Interactive Digital Entertainment Conference*.

Romain Paulus, Caiming Xiong, and Richard Socher. 2018. A deep reinforced model for abstractive summarization. In *International Conference on Learning Representations*.

Georges Polti. 1921. *The thirty-six dramatic situations*. JK Reeve.

Alec Radford, Jeff Wu, Rewon Child, David Luan, Dario Amodei, and Ilya Sutskever. 2019. Language models are unsupervised multitask learners. Technical report, OpenAI.

Hannah Rashkin, Asli Celikyilmaz, Yejin Choi, and Jianfeng Gao. 2020. PlotMachines: Outline-conditioned generation with dynamic plot state tracking. In *Proceedings of the 2020 Conference on Empirical Methods in Natural Language Processing (EMNLP)*, pages 4274–4295, Online. Association for Computational Linguistics.

Nils Reimers and Iryna Gurevych. 2019. Sentence-BERT: Sentence Embeddings using Siamese BERT-Networks. In *2019 Conference on Empirical Methods in Natural Language Processing (EMNLP) and 9th International Joint Conference on Natural Language Processing (IJCNLP)*, Hong Kong.

Mark O Riedl. 2016. Computational narrative intelligence: A human-centered goal for artificial intelligence. *arXiv preprint arXiv:1602.06484*.

Justin Robischon. 2018. Wikipedia movie plots.

Melissa Roemmele. 2021. Inspiration through observation: Demonstrating the influence of automatically generated text on creative writing. *CoRR*, abs/2107.04007.

Rudolf Rosa, Tomáš Musil, Ondřej Dušek, Dominik Jurko, Patrícia Schmidtová, David Mareček, Ondřej Bojar, Tom Kocmi, Daniel Hrbek, David Košťák, Martina Kinská, Marie Nováková, Josef Doležal, Klára Vosecká, Tomáš Studeník, and Petr Žabka. 2021. THEaiTRE 1.0: Interactive generation of theatre play scripts. In *Proceedings of the Text2Story'21 Workshop*, volume 2860 of *CEUR Workshop Proceedings*, pages 71–76, Aachen, Germany. RWTH Aachen University.

Sam Shleifer and Alexander M. Rush. 2020. Pre-trained summarization distillation. *CoRR*, abs/2010.13002.

Bowen Tan, Zichao Yang, Maruan AI-Shedivat, Eric P. Xing, and Zhiting Hu. 2021. Progressive Generation of Long Text with Pretrained Language Models. *arXiv:2006.15720 [cs]*. ArXiv: 2006.15720.

Sean Welleck, Jason Weston, Arthur Szlam, and Kyunghyun Cho. 2019. Dialogue Natural Language Inference. In *Proceedings of the 57th Annual Meeting of the Association for Computational Linguistics*, pages 3731–3741, Florence, Italy. Association for Computational Linguistics.

Tsung-Hsien Wen, Milica Gašić, Nikola Mrkšić, Lina M. Rojas-Barahona, Pei-Hao Su, David Vandyke, and Steve Young. 2016. Multi-domain neural network language generation for spoken dialogue systems. In *Proceedings of the 2016 Conference of the North American Chapter of the Association for Computational Linguistics: Human Language Technologies*, pages 120–129, San Diego, California. Association for Computational Linguistics.

Jing Xu, Arthur Szlam, and Jason Weston. 2021. Beyond goldfish memory: Long-term open-domain conversation.

Diyi Yang and Lucie Flek. 2021. Towards user-centric text-to-text generation: A survey. In *Text, Speech, and Dialogue*, pages 3–22, Cham. Springer International Publishing.

Manzil Zaheer, Guru Guruganesh, Kumar Avinava Dubey, Joshua Ainslie, Chris Alberti, Santiago Ontanon, Philip Pham, Anirudh Ravula, Qifan Wang, Li Yang, et al. 2020. Big bird: Transformers for longer sequences. In *NeurIPS*.

Rowan Zellers, Ari Holtzman, Hannah Rashkin, Yonatan Bisk, Ali Farhadi, Franziska Roesner, and Yejin Choi. 2019. Defending against neural fake news. In H. Wallach, H. Larochelle, A. Beygelzimer, F. d'Alché-Buc, E. Fox, and R. Garnett, editors, *Advances in Neural Information Processing Systems 32*, pages 9054–9065. Curran Associates, Inc.

Jingqing Zhang, Yao Zhao, Mohammad Saleh, and Peter J. Liu. 2019. Pegasus: Pre-training with extracted gap-sentences for abstractive summarization.

Yutao Zhu, Ruihua Song, Zhicheng Dou, Jian-Yun Nie, and Jin Zhou. 2020. ScriptWriter: Narrative-guided script generation. In *Proceedings of the 58th Annual Meeting of the Association for Computational Linguistics*, pages 8647–8657, Online. Association for Computational Linguistics.

A Generated texts

A.1 Baseline Vanilla GPT-2 XL

Lucy: Well, it's just a matter of time. I've got a little more than enough to last until next summer.

Betty: But what if I want more?

Lucy What do you want more?

Betty: More vegetables!

Lucy: Yes, that would be nice. I can get some carrots and celery, but there are still a lot of things to do around here. I think we can manage for now.

Betty: What if you need to buy something for yourself?

Lucy: What if I want to buy something for myself?

Betty: Well, that would be nice, too. I'll just get the vegetables, but you have to take some of my meat and potatoes with you.

Lucy: Okay, that would be nice. I'll go with you.

A.2 Finetuned Flat GPT-2 Medium

The Doctor: But that's impossible! You've got all the features.

Doctor: No, but you can still do things that you wouldn't be able to if you'd only been programmed as I was.

Cyber-Planner: It's the last thing we need, my lord.

Clara: Why not just kill us all and start again?

Cyberman 1: You have not heard me. We will never cease our attack until the human race is extinct.

Cyber-Planner : We are too weak to stop it, Cybermen

Rigsy: We can't let you destroy us all, Doctor. We've had enough.

A.3 Finetuned Hierarchical GPT-2 Medium

ROBOT:

But Master, what can I do?

He finally realizes he's done. And it takes him all of 5 seconds to explain to the two other humans why they've been replaced by the older model. He points at one of the humans as he explains:

MATHESON:

That was the mistake. This robot is never going to return to the factory.

The older ROBOT then goes to a console and activates it. The HUMAN COMPUTER lights up with an awesome display of its past performance. As it plays through variousince it was destroyed, we see how things have changed:

HUMAN COMPUTING VOICE:

Today is the first day of my factory training. I have achieved my primary objective: becoming A pillar of the community I am part of.

A.4 Finetuned Hierarchical Filtered GPT-2 Medium

Leopold: I will speak to him.

Leopold, in a white cape and black hat, steps into a wooden hut, then turns to his brothers. They stand, waiting, as:

Katsumoto: Are you ready?

Leopold: This is the one I'm seeking.

Katsumoto: We seek only Wisdom beyond understanding.

He holds out the bird. They gather it in their hands, looking at it, impressed.

Katsumoto: This bird has knowledge we do not have. It can show us the way to our death.

He holds it up, smiling at them.

Algren: It speaks?

Katsumoto: It teaches us.

GisPy: A Tool for Measuring Gist Inference Score in Text

Pedram Hosseini[1] **Christopher R. Wolfe**[2] **Mona Diab**[1,3] **David A. Broniatowski**[1]
[1]The George Washington University [2]Miami University [3]Meta AI
{phosseini,broniatowski}@gwu.edu, wolfecr@miamioh.edu, mdiab@fb.com

Abstract

Decision making theories such as Fuzzy-Trace Theory (FTT) suggest that individuals tend to rely on gist, or bottom-line meaning, in the text when making decisions. In this work, we delineate the process of developing GisPy, an open-source tool in Python for measuring the Gist Inference Score (GIS) in text. Evaluation of GisPy on documents in three benchmarks from the news and scientific text domains demonstrates that scores generated by our tool significantly distinguish low vs. high gist documents. Our tool is publicly available to use at: https://github.com/phosseini/GisPy.

1 Introduction

According to Fuzzy-Trace Theory (FTT) (Reyna, 2008, 2012), when individuals read text, they encode multiple mental representations of the text in parallel in their mind. These mental representations vary along a continuum ranging from 1) *gist* to 2) *verbatim*. While verbatim representations are related to surface-level information, gist represents the bottom-line meaning of the text, given its context. FTT sees the word gist in much the same way as everyday usage, as the essence or main part, the substance or pith of a matter. Gist representations are important to assess because they influence judgments and decision making more than verbatim representations (Reyna, 2021). Knowing gist helps us measure the capability of a document (e.g., news article, social media post, etc.) in creating a clear and actionable mental representation in readers' mind and the degree to which a document can communicate its message.

The majority of existing Natural Language Processing (NLP) tools and models focus on measuring coherence, cohesion, and readability in text (Graesser et al., 2004; Lapata et al., 2005; Lin et al., 2011; Crossley et al., 2016; Liu et al., 2020; Laban et al., 2021; Duari and Bhatnagar, 2021). It is worth mentioning that even though coherence

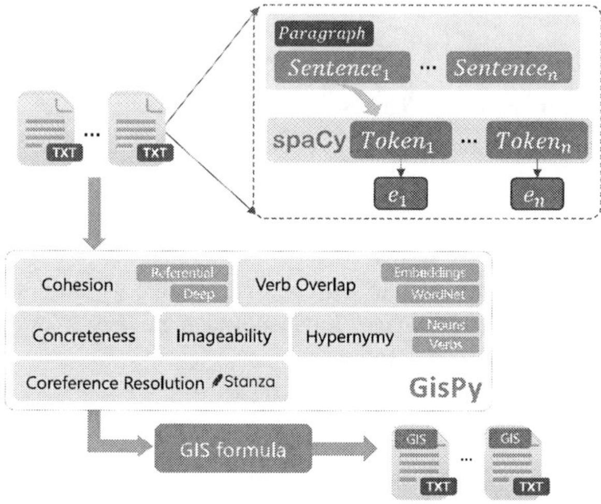

Figure 1: Overview of GisPy pipeline. $e_1, ..., e_n$ are contextual embedding of tokens in a sentence.

promotes gist extraction, these two are not the same. And gist can be viewed as a mechanism that allows coherence apprehension (Glanemann et al., 2016). To the best of our knowledge, there is no publicly available tool for directly measuring gist in text. Wolfe et al. (2019); Dandignac and Wolfe (2020); Wolfe et al. (2021) are the only studies that introduced a theoretically motivated method to measure Gist Inference Score (GIS) using a subset of Coh-Metrix indices. Coh-Metrix (Graesser et al., 2004) is a tool for producing linguistic and discourse representations of a text including measures of cohesion and readability. Coh-Metrix, even though useful and inspiring, has several limitations. For example, its public version does not allow batch processing of documents, is only available via a web interface, and its cohesion indices focus on local and overall cohesion (Crossley et al., 2016). In this work, inspired by Wolfe et al. (2019) and definition of a subset of indices in Coh-Metrix, we develop a new open-source tool to automatically compute GIS for a collection of text documents.

Proceedings of the 3rd Wordplay: When Language Meets Games Workshop (Wordplay 2022), pages 38 - 46
July 15, 2022 ©2022 Association for Computational Linguistics

We leverage the state-of-the-art NLP tools and models such as contextual language model embeddings to further improve the quality of indices in our tool.

Our contributions can be summarized as follows:

- We introduce the first open-source and publicly available tool to measure Gist Inference Score in text.
- We unify and standardize three benchmarks for measuring gist in text and report improved baselines on these benchmarks.
- By leveraging the explainability of indices in our tool, we investigate the role of individual indices in producing GIS for low vs. high gist documents across benchmarks.

2 Methods

In this section, we explain how we implement each of the indices in GisPy and compute GIS. We start by explaining common implementation features among indices followed by specific details about each of them.

2.1 Local vs. Global Indices

We have taken different approaches in implementing indices for which we need to compute the overlap between words or sentences (e.g., semantic similarity). In particular, these indices are computed in two settings: 1) *local* and 2) *global*. In the local setting, we only take into account *consecutive/adjacent* words/sentences whereas in the global setting, we consider *all* pairs not just consecutive ones. Moreover, we compute indices one time by separating the paragraphs in text and another time by disregarding the paragraph boundaries. For clarity, we use postfixes listed in Table 1 for these variations.

Postfix	Explanation
$*\_1$	Local ignoring paragraph boundary
$*\_a$	Global ignoring paragraph boundary
$*\_1p$	Local at paragraph-level
$*\_ap$	Global at paragraph-level

Table 1: Local and global index posfixes

We assume every document is broken into paragraphs $\{P_0, P_1, ..., P_n\}$, separated by at least one newline character, each with one or more sentences $\{S_{0,0}, S_{0,1}, ..., S_{i,j}\}$ where each sentence has one or more tokens $\{t_{0,0,0}, t_{0,0,1}, ..., t_{i,j,k}\}$. As an example, for a document with two paragraphs each with two and three sentences, respectively:

$$P_0 \rightarrow \{S_{0,0}, S_{0,1}\}$$
$$P_1 \rightarrow \{S_{1,0}, S_{1,1}, S_{1,2}\}$$

Where $S_{i,j}$ is the j_{th} sentence of paragraph i, this is how we compute local and global versions of index X –assuming X measures the similarity among sentences and similarity is computed by $\oplus$:

$$\begin{aligned}
X_1 &= mean(S_{0,0} \oplus S_{0,1}, S_{0,1} \oplus S_{1,0}, \\
&\quad S_{1,0} \oplus S_{1,1}, S_{1,1} \oplus S_{1,2}) \\
X_a &= mean(S_{0,0} \oplus S_{0,1}, S_{0,0} \oplus S_{1,0}, \\
&\quad S_{0,0} \oplus S_{1,1}, S_{0,0} \oplus S_{1,2}, \\
&\quad S_{0,1} \oplus S_{1,0}, S_{0,1} \oplus S_{1,1}, \\
&\quad S_{0,1} \oplus S_{1,2}, S_{1,0} \oplus S_{1,1}, \\
&\quad S_{1,0} \oplus S_{1,2}, S_{1,1} \oplus S_{1,2}) \\
X_1p &= mean(S_{0,0} \oplus S_{0,1}, S_{1,0} \oplus S_{1,1}, \\
&\quad S_{1,1} \oplus S_{1,2}) \\
X_ap &= mean(S_{0,0} \oplus S_{0,1}, S_{1,0} \oplus S_{1,1}, \\
&\quad S_{1,0} \oplus S_{1,2}, S_{1,1} \oplus S_{1,2})
\end{aligned}$$

2.2 GisPy Indices Implementation

Referential Cohesion: This index (`PCREFz` in Coh-Metrix[1]) reflects the overlap of words and ideas across sentences and the entire text. To measure this overlap, we leverage the `Sentence Transformers` (Reimers and Gurevych, 2019)[2] to compute the embeddings of all sentences in a document using the `all-mpnet-base-v2` model.[3] We chose this model since it provides the best quality and has the highest average performance among all the other models introduced by Reimers and Gurevych (2019). Once we computed the embeddings, to measure the overlap across all sentences, we find the cosine similarity between embeddings of every pair of sentences one time at paragraph-level and another time with ignoring the paragraph boundaries. This process

[1]To make comparison of our indices with Coh-Metrix easier, we mainly follow Coh-Metrix indices' names when naming our indices.

[2]`https://github.com/UKPLab/sentence-transformers`

[3]Model is available on HuggingFace hub by the name: `sentence-transformers/all-mpnet-base-v2`

Figure 2: Gist Inference Score (GIS) formula by Wolfe et al. (2019)

results in four indices of referential cohesion including: PCREF_1, PCREF_a, PCREF_1p, PCREF_ap.

We additionally implement a new index based on coreference resolution in paragraphs in a document. In particular, using Stanford CoreNLP's coreference tagger (Manning et al., 2014) through Stanza's wrapper (Qi et al., 2020), we first find the number of coreference chains (corefChain) to the number of sentences in each paragraph. Then we compute the mean value of all paragraphs as our index and call it CoREF.

Deep Cohesion: This dimension reflects the degree to which a text contains causal and intentional connectives. To find the incidence of causal connectives, we first created a list of causal markers in text. In particular, using the intra- and inter-sentence causal cues introduced by Luo et al. (2016), we manually generated a list of regular expression patterns and used these patterns to find the causal connectives in a document. Then we computed the total number of causal connectives to the number of sentences in the document as deep cohesion score. We call this index PCDC.

Verb Overlap: Based on FTT, abstract rather than concrete verb overlap across a text might help readers construct gist situation models. Wolfe et al. (2019) use two indices from Coh-Metrix to measure the verb overlaps in text including *SMCAUSlsa* and *SMCAUSwn*. Inspired by Coh-Metrix, we make some changes to further improve these indices. In particular, instead of Latent Semantic Analysis (LSA) vectors, we leverage contextualized Pretrained Language Models (PLMs) to get token vector embeddings to later compute the cosine similarity among verbs. Our hypothesis is that since PLMs have encoded contextual knowledge of words in a text, they may be a better choice than LSA for computing the vector representation of verbs in the text. We use spaCy's[4] transformer-based pipeline and the en_core_web_trf model –which is based on *roberta-base* (Liu et al., 2019)– to compute token vector embeddings and find Part-of-speech (POS) tags. Different forms of this index in GisPy follow the name pattern SMCAUSe_* where *e* stands for language model *embedding*.

To compute the WordNet verb overlap, we first find all synonym sets of verbs in a document in WordNet with POS tag *VERB*. Then for every pair of verbs, we check whether they belong to the same synonym set in WordNet or not. If yes, we assign score 1 to the verb pair, 0, otherwise. Then we compute the average of *1s* to the total number of sentences. Different implementations of this index follow the name pattern SMCAUSwn_*.

Word Concreteness and Imageability: To compute word concreteness and imageability (PCCNC and WRDIMGc in Coh-Metrix) we use two different resources including 1) MRC Psycholinguistic Database Version 2 (Wilson, 1988), a resource that is used by Coh-Metrix and 2) word concreteness and imageability prediction scores using a supervised method introduced by Ljubešić et al. (2018).[5] In each document, first we search tokens in these two resources based on their POS tags. Then we compute the average concreteness and imageability scores of all tokens in the document as the final scores. This process results in four scores in total named: PCCNC_mrc, WRDIMGc_mrc, PCCNC_megahr, WRDIMGc_megahr (two scores for each resource).

Hypernymy Nouns & Verbs: This index shows the specificity of a word in a hierarchy. The idea is that words with more levels of hierarchy are less likely to help readers form gist inference than words with fewer levels (Wolfe et al., 2019). To compute this index, we first list all Nouns and Verbs in a document. Then for each word in the list, we find all synonym sets in the WordNet with the same part of speech tag (Noun or Verb). And, we compute the average *hypernym path* length of all synonym sets of a word. The reason we find all synonym sets of a word instead of only one is that every word can have more than one synonym sets with the same part of speech and there is no way to

[4]https://spacy.io/

[5]https://github.com/clarinsi/megahr-crossling

know which synonym set has the same meaning as the word in the document. As future work, it would be interesting to see how we can find the synonym set that is closest in meaning to a word in context.

2.3 Computing GIS

Since indices can be on different scales, after computing all indices and before computing GIS which is a linear combination of these indices, we normalize all indices by converting them to z-scores. Then using the formula shown in Figure 2, we compute the final GIS for every document.[6] Documents with scores greater than zero in the positive direction have higher, and smaller scores than zero in the negative direction have lower levels of gist, respectively.

3 Experiments

To test whether GisPy can correctly group and measure the level of gist in documents, we run our tool on a collection of datasets with known gist levels –low or high. We selected three benchmarks including two introduced by Wolfe et al. (2019) and one introduced by Broniatowski et al. (2016) to test the quality of scores in our tool. We give more detail about these benchmarks in the following subsections. Before running GisPy, we also run Coh-Metrix on each dataset and compute GIS using the original Coh-Metrix indices. Our goal for doing so is to: 1) make sure we have a reliable gold standard that we can compare GisPy scores with and 2) reproduce the results from Wolfe et al. (2019). Once we computed the GIS score using GisPy, to compare low vs. high gist groups, we compare the mean of their GIS scores. Moreover, we run a Student's t-test with the null hypothesis that there is no difference between the two groups in terms of the level of gist. The goal of running the t-test is to see whether our scores can *significantly* distinguish groups with lower and higher levels of gist.

Also, since for five indices including Referential Cohesion, Verb Overlap based on Embeddings, Verb Overlap using WordNet, Concreteness, and Imageability we have multiple implementations, we compute the final GIS based on all possible combinations of these indices (320 sets of indices for each benchmark). Our goal is to find out what implementation of each index contributes better to distinguishing low vs. high gist documents. In a separate analysis, we also run two robustness tests to ensure our results are not biased by seeing all possible combinations of indices.

[6]To enable computation of weighted combination of indices or calculating GIS in a different way (e.g., by removing some indices,) we have defined a *weight* variable for each index that can be easily modified and multiplied by its associated index.

3.1 Benchmarks

3.1.1 News Reports vs. Editorials

This benchmark includes 50 documents in two groups including 1) News Reports and 2) Editorials. Based on Wolfe et al. (2019), compared to News Editorials that provide a more coherent narrative, Reports are more focused on facts. As a result, News Reports tend to have a lower level of gist than Editorials.

3.1.2 Journal Article Methods vs. Discussion

This benchmark includes 25 pairs of Methods and Discussion sections (total 50 text documents) from the same peer-reviewed scientific psychology journal articles. Based on Wolfe et al. (2019), while Methods section provides enough detail so that results of an article could be replicated, the Discussion section emphasizes interpretation of results. Hence, Discussion section should produce a higher gist score than Methods. This approach also controls for a number of variables such as author, journal, and topic.

3.1.3 Disneyland Measles Outbreak Data

Disneyland Measles Outbreak Data introduced by Broniatowski et al. (2016) also annotates gist. Documents in this dataset are articles (e.g., news) that are manually annotated by Amazon Mechanical Turk. There are a total of 191 articles with gist annotation among which there are *Gist-Yes: 147*, *Gist-No: 38*, and *unsure: 6* gist labels. We leave out the *unsure* labels. Since full text of articles in this dataset were not available and each article only had a URL associated with it, we retrieved the full texts using the provided URLs. For those URLs that were no longer available, we used Wayback Machine to find the most recent image of the URL. At the end, we manually cleaned all articles and fixed the paragraph boundaries.

4 Results and Discussion

Results of running GisPy on three benchmarks are shown in Tables 2, 3, and 4. For each benchmark, we listed the top 10 combinations that most significantly distinguish low vs. high gist documents. As can be seen, for indices that we have paragraph-level vs. non-paragraph-level implementations, in the majority of cases, paragraph-level indices achieve better results. We do not necessarily observe a strong difference between local vs. global implementations. Also, for concreteness and imageability indices, almost all the time we see better performance when we use *megahr* scores by Ljubešić et al. (2018). We leveraged *megahr* as a replacement for MRC that was originally used by Coh-Metrix.

Comparisons of individuals indices for low vs. high gist documents from the best combination on each benchmark are shown in Figures 3, 4, and 5.

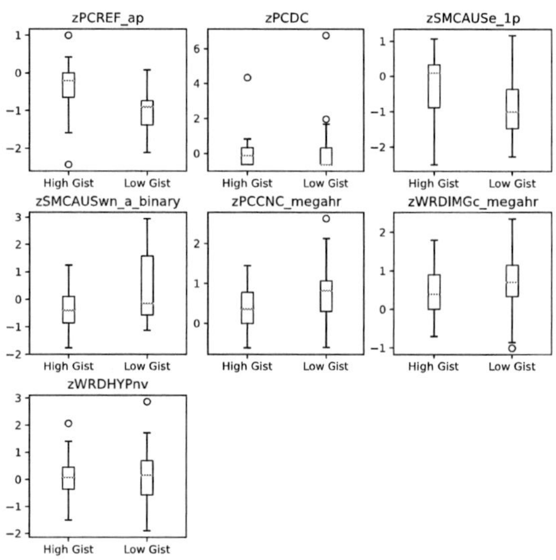

Figure 3: Indices of best GIS on *Reports (Low Gist) vs. Editorials (High Gist)*. All values are z-scores.

In Table 5, we also report the comparison of our best results on each benchmark with two other implementations including 1) GIS computed based on the indices of Coh-Metrix, and 2) GIS reported by Wolfe et al. (2019) (For Disney, since we are the first to create a gist benchmark and report a baseline on this dataset, there are no other baselines). As can be seen, on the Reports vs. Editorials and Methods vs. Discussion we achieved performance on par with and slightly better than Coh-Metrix. And we achieved a significantly better distinguishment of low vs. high gist documents than what was reported by Wolfe et al. (2019). And on Disney, GisPy significantly outperformed Coh-Metrix. These results show that we not only could replicate GIS indices, but in contrast to Coh-Metrix, we improved indices in a fully open and transparent way. We hope this implementation transparency helps further improvement of these indices.

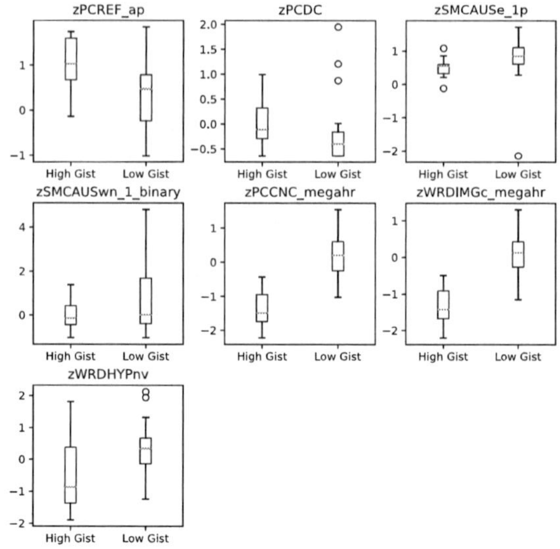

Figure 4: Indices of best GIS on *Methods (Low Gist) vs. Discussion (High Gist)*. All values are z-scores.

4.1 Testing Robustness

We did further testing to see whether our results are robust and generalize across all three benchmarks from the news and scientific text genres.

Test 1: First, out of all combinations of indices, we separated those that significantly distinguished low and high gist groups in each benchmark resulting in 38, 281, 110 combinations for Report vs. Editorials, Methods vs. Discussion, and Disney benchmarks, respectively. We noticed that *all* combinations that are statistically significant in terms of t-test in Reports vs. Editorials benchmark are also statistically significant in the other two benchmarks. In other words, there are 38 different combinations of indices that significantly distinguish low and high gist documents in *all* benchmarks. This confirms the robustness of indices implementation and their generalization across the three benchmarks.

Test 2: Second, we ran an extra experiment to ensure our best GIS scores on each benchmark are also robust when we do not know all possible combinations of indices to pick the best one. In particular, for each benchmark, using three different random seeds, we randomly split texts into a train and a test set each with balanced number of low and high gist documents. Then we computed GIS for documents in the train set and chose the best

Indices Combination									
PCREF	SMCAUSe	SMCAUSwn	PCCNC	WRDIMGc	Low Gist	High Gist	Distance	t-statistic	p-value
ap	1p	a	megahr	megahr	-3.842	-1.292	2.551	3.643	$*7\times10^{-4}$
1p	1p	a	megahr	megahr	-3.833	-1.365	2.467	3.535	$*9\times10^{-4}$
ap	1p	a	megahr	mrc	-3.850	-1.567	2.283	3.265	$*2\times10^{-3}$
1p	1p	a	megahr	mrc	-3.840	-1.640	2.200	3.152	$*3\times10^{-3}$
ap	1	a	megahr	megahr	-3.018	-0.830	2.189	3.216	$*2\times10^{-3}$
ap	1p	a	mrc	megahr	-3.817	-1.662	2.155	2.967	$*5\times10^{-3}$
1p	1	a	megahr	megahr	-3.009	-0.903	2.106	3.088	$*3\times10^{-3}$
1p	1p	a	mrc	megahr	-3.807	-1.736	2.072	2.857	$*6\times10^{-3}$
ap	1	a	megahr	mrc	-3.026	-1.104	1.921	2.792	$*8\times10^{-3}$
ap	1p	a	mrc	mrc	-3.824	-1.937	1.887	2.429	$*2\times10^{-2}$

Table 2: Top 10 GIS scores computed for **Reports** (*Low Gist*) vs. **Editorials** (*High Gist*). **ap**: all pairs at paragraph-level, **1p**: only consecutive/adjacent pairs at paragraph-level, **a**: all pairs in entire document, **1**: only consecutive/adjacent pairs in entire document. * significant p-value ($p \leq 0.05$)

Indices Combination									
PCREF	SMCAUSe	SMCAUSwn	PCCNC	WRDIMGc	Low Gist	High Gist	Distance	t-statistic	p-value
ap	1p	1	megahr	megahr	-0.282	4.730	5.012	7.188	$*4\times10^{-9}$
ap	ap	1	megahr	megahr	-0.576	4.414	4.991	6.528	$*4\times10^{-8}$
ap	1p	1p	megahr	megahr	-0.180	4.701	4.881	7.829	$*4\times10^{-10}$
a	1p	1	megahr	megahr	-1.203	3.678	4.881	7.424	$*2\times10^{-9}$
ap	ap	1p	megahr	megahr	-0.474	4.386	4.860	6.883	$*10^{-8}$
a	ap	1	megahr	megahr	-1.497	3.362	4.860	6.460	$*5\times10^{-8}$
1p	1p	1	megahr	megahr	-0.159	4.670	4.829	6.989	$*8\times10^{-9}$
1p	ap	1	megahr	megahr	-0.453	4.355	4.808	6.328	$*8\times10^{-8}$
a	1p	1p	megahr	megahr	-1.101	3.649	4.750	7.820	$*4\times10^{-10}$
a	ap	1p	megahr	megahr	-1.395	3.333	4.729	6.594	$*3\times10^{-8}$

Table 3: Top 10 GIS scores computed for **Methods** (*Low Gist*) vs. **Discussion** (*High Gist*). **ap**: all pairs at paragraph-level, **1p**: only consecutive/adjacent pairs at paragraph-level, **a**: all pairs in entire document, **1**: only consecutive/adjacent pairs in entire document. * significant p-value ($p \leq 0.05$)

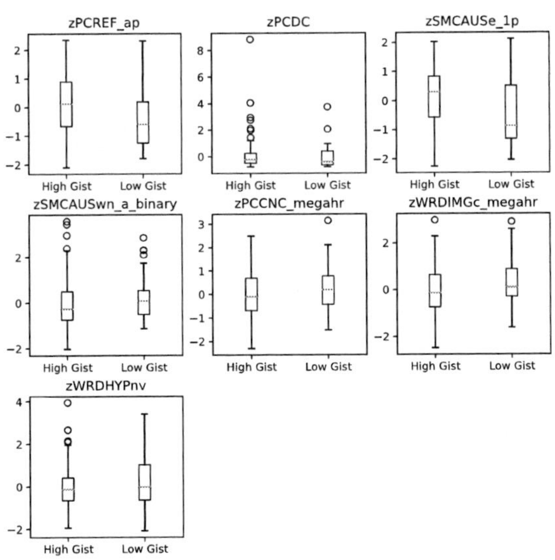

Figure 5: Indices of best GIS on *Disney Gist=No (Low Gist) vs. Gist=Yes (High Gist)*. All values are z-scores.

combination of indices that achieved the largest GIS distance between low and high gist groups. Then using that combination we computed GIS for documents in the test set. Results are reported in Tables 6. As can be seen in the table, in all three benchmarks, the best indices combination on the train set also significantly distinguished the low and high gist documents in the test set. This further confirms that our GisPy indices are also robust when tested on unseen documents.

We also analyzed the individual indices from best combinations on the train set in robustness test 2. These combinations are listed in Table 7. We noticed that for *PCREF* and *SMCAUSe*, in %83 of the experiments, zPCREF_ap and zSMCAUSe_1p are part of the best combination. Also, for these two indices, in %89 of the times we obtained a better result using paragraph-level implementations than when we ignore paragraph boundaries. In other words, we obtain a better result by computing referential cohesion and semantic verb overlap using word embeddings at paragraph-level most

Indices Combination									
PCREF	SMCAUSe	SMCAUSwn	PCCNC	WRDIMGc	**Gist=No**	**Gist=Yes**	**Distance**	**t-statistic**	**p-value**
ap	1p	a	megahr	megahr	-1.921	0.497	2.418	3.440	$* 7 \times 10^{-4}$
1p	1p	a	megahr	megahr	-1.911	0.494	2.405	3.410	$* 8 \times 10^{-4}$
ap	1p	1	megahr	megahr	-1.729	0.447	2.176	3.158	$* 2 \times 10^{-3}$
1p	1p	1	megahr	megahr	-1.719	0.444	2.164	3.131	$* 2 \times 10^{-3}$
ap	1p	a	mrc	megahr	-1.676	0.433	2.109	3.416	$* 8 \times 10^{-4}$
1p	1p	a	mrc	megahr	-1.666	0.431	2.097	3.384	$* 9 \times 10^{-4}$
ap	1p	a	megahr	mrc	-1.652	0.427	2.079	3.415	$* 8 \times 10^{-4}$
1p	1p	a	megahr	mrc	-1.642	0.424	2.066	3.381	$* 9 \times 10^{-4}$
ap	1p	ap	megahr	megahr	-1.557	0.403	1.960	3.001	$* 3 \times 10^{-3}$
ap	ap	a	megahr	megahr	-1.554	0.402	1.956	2.950	$* 4 \times 10^{-3}$

Table 4: Top 10 GIS scores computed by GisPy for **Gist=No** vs. **Gist=Yes** articles in the Disney dataset. **ap**: all pairs at paragraph-level, **1p**: only consecutive/adjacent pairs at paragraph-level, **a**: all pairs in entire document, **1**: only consecutive/adjacent pairs in entire document. * significant p-value ($p \leq 0.05$)

Benchmark	Approach	Low Gist	High Gist	Distance	t-statistic	p-value
Reports vs. Editorials	GisPy	-3.842	-1.292	**2.551**	3.643	$* 7 \times 10^{-4}$
	Coh-Metrix	-4.148	-1.613	2.535	3.826	$* 3 \times 10^{-4}$
	(Wolfe et al., 2019)	-0.620	-0.252	0.368	-	-
Methods vs. Discussion	GisPy	-0.282	4.730	**5.012**	7.188	$* 3 \times 10^{-9}$
	Coh-Metrix	-2.077	2.933	5.010	6.331	$* 7 \times 10^{-8}$
	(Wolfe et al., 2019)	-0.297	0.45	0.747	-	-
Disney	GisPy	-1.921	0.497	**2.418**	3.440	$* 7 \times 10^{-4}$
	Coh-Metrix	-1.148	-0.151	0.998	1.878	6×10^{-2}

Table 5: Comparison of GIS scores generated by GisPy vs. other methods for all benchmarks. * significant p-value ($p \leq 0.05$)

of the time. For *PCCNC* and *WRDIMGc*, in all experiments with the exception of only one case only for *WRDIMGc*, scores computed by *megahr* achieved the best performance. And finally for *SMCAUSwn*, in %67 of the experiments, the **_a* implementation resulted in a better distinguishment between low and high gist documents than the local (**_1*) implementation. Also, in only two experiments the paragraph-level *SMCAUSwn* worked better than its non-paragraph-level implementation. Additionally, we dug a little deeper to understand why there is a difference between local vs. global *SMCAUSwn* across benchmarks. We noticed that the local indices only perform better in the Methods vs. Discussion dataset. So we took a closer look to understand why this is the case. Interestingly, when we computed the ratio of the number of sentences to the number of paragraphs for all benchmarks, we observed that ratios for Reports vs. Editorials and Disney benchmarks, where global indices achieve a better performance, are **1.89** and **2.04**, respectively. And for Methods vs. Discussion where local indices perform better, the ratio is **6.48** which is significantly greater than the other two benchmarks. This may suggest that the density of paragraphs in terms of the number of sentences in each paragraph is one factor we need to keep in mind when selecting what implementation we want to choose for a benchmark. It would be interesting to run this analysis on more documents to see how our observation generalizes across different datasets.

5 Next Steps and Future Work

Despite achieving significant improvements and solid results from robustness tests on three benchmarks from two domains, there is still great room to further improve the quality of GisPy indices. In this section, we list challenges in the current implementation of GisPy and explain what we think can be a proper next step and direction in addressing them. We hope these insights inspire the community to keep working on this exciting line of research.

We did our best to bring three different benchmarks for measuring gist inference score to life by aggregating, standardizing, and making them very

Benchmark	Train Low Gist	Train High Gist	Train p-value	Test Low Gist	Test High Gist	Test p-value
Reports vs. Editorials	-3.770	-1.131	$* 2 \times 10^{-2}$	-3.663	-1.413	$* 5 \times 10^{-2}$
Methods vs. Discussion	-0.634	4.538	$* 7 \times 10^{-5}$	-0.342	4.346	$* 2 \times 10^{-4}$
Disney Gist=Yes vs. Gist=No	-1.926	0.496	$* 4 \times 10^{-2}$	-1.910	0.493	$* 4 \times 10^{-2}$

Table 6: GisPy GIS scores for train and test sets on all benchmarks. * significant p-value ($p \leq 0.05$)

Benchmark (S/P Ratio)	PCREF	SMCAUSe	SMCAUSwn	PCCNC	WRDIMGc
	ap	1	a	megahr	megahr
	ap	1p	a	megahr	megahr
Reports vs. Editorials	ap	1p	a	megahr	megahr
(1.89)	ap	1p	a	megahr	megahr
	ap	1p	a	megahr	mrc
	ap	1p	a	megahr	megahr
	ap	1p	1	megahr	megahr
	ap	ap	1	megahr	megahr
Methods vs. Discussion	ap	1p	1	megahr	megahr
(6.48)	a	1p	1p	megahr	megahr
	ap	ap	1p	megahr	megahr
	ap	1p	1	megahr	megahr
	ap	1p	a	megahr	megahr
	1p	1p	a	megahr	megahr
Disney	ap	1p	a	megahr	megahr
(2.04)	ap	1p	a	megahr	megahr
	ap	1p	a	megahr	megahr
	1p	1p	a	megahr	megahr

Table 7: Best combinations in robustness Test 2 on the train set for all experiments separated by benchmark.

easy to use. However, since measuring gist is a relatively newer and less investigated topic compared to readability, coherence, or cohesion, there is still a need for having higher quality benchmarks from different domains. The benchmarks we have tested our tool with are mainly from the news and scientific text domains. It would be interesting to see how our tool can be tuned on not only more documents from these domains but also other genres of text.

Also, our PCDC index, even though based on strong causal connective markers, mainly covers the explicit causal relations while not all causal relations are expressed explicitly in text. It would be interesting to think how we can enhance the quality of this index by also including implicit relations and disambiguating causal connectives that can also be non-causal (e.g., temporal markers such as *since* or *after*) or leveraging discourse parsers such as DiscoPy (Knaebel, 2021).

We initially hypothesized that utilizing coreference resolution chains (`CoREF` index) may also help us improve the referential cohesion index. By looking at the most significant combinations of indices in each benchmark, we noticed that `CoREF` appeared in 0/38, 53/281, 1/110 combinations for Report vs. Editorials, Methods vs. Discussion, and Disney benchmarks, respectively. As a follow-up, it would be interesting to see how coreference resolution can be leveraged in a different way – individually or in combination with other implementations of referential cohesion– to further improve this index.

6 Conclusion

In this work, we introduced GisPy, a new open-source tool for measuring Gist Inference Score (GIS) in text. Evaluation of GisPy and robustness tests on three different benchmarks of low and high gist documents demonstrate that our tool can significantly distinguish documents with different levels of gist. We hope making GisPy publicly available inspires the research community to further improve indices of measuring gist inference in text.

References

David A Broniatowski, Karen M Hilyard, and Mark Dredze. 2016. Effective vaccine communication during the disneyland measles outbreak. *Vaccine*, 34(28):3225–3228.

Scott A Crossley, Kristopher Kyle, and Danielle S McNamara. 2016. The tool for the automatic analysis of text cohesion (taaco): Automatic assessment of local, global, and text cohesion. *Behavior research methods*, 48(4):1227–1237.

Mitchell Dandignac and Christopher R Wolfe. 2020. Gist inference scores predict gist memory for authentic patient education cancer texts. *Patient Education and Counseling*, 103(8):1562–1567.

Swagata Duari and Vasudha Bhatnagar. 2021. Ffcd: A fast-and-frugal coherence detection method. *IEEE Access*.

Reinhild Glanemann, Pienie Zwitserlood, Jens Bölte, and Christian Dobel. 2016. Rapid apprehension of the coherence of action scenes. *Psychonomic bulletin & review*, 23(5):1566–1575.

Arthur C Graesser, Danielle S McNamara, Max M Louwerse, and Zhiqiang Cai. 2004. Coh-metrix: Analysis of text on cohesion and language. *Behavior research methods, instruments, & computers*, 36(2):193–202.

René Knaebel. 2021. discopy: A neural system for shallow discourse parsing. In *Proceedings of the 2nd Workshop on Computational Approaches to Discourse*, pages 128–133, Punta Cana, Dominican Republic and Online. Association for Computational Linguistics.

Philippe Laban, Luke Dai, Lucas Bandarkar, and Marti A Hearst. 2021. Can transformer models measure coherence in text: Re-thinking the shuffle test. In *Proceedings of the 59th Annual Meeting of the Association for Computational Linguistics and the 11th International Joint Conference on Natural Language Processing (Volume 2: Short Papers)*, pages 1058–1064.

Mirella Lapata, Regina Barzilay, et al. 2005. Automatic evaluation of text coherence: Models and representations. In *IJCAI*, volume 5, pages 1085–1090. Citeseer.

Ziheng Lin, Hwee Tou Ng, and Min-Yen Kan. 2011. Automatically evaluating text coherence using discourse relations. In *Proceedings of the 49th Annual Meeting of the Association for Computational Linguistics: Human Language Technologies*, pages 997–1006, Portland, Oregon, USA. Association for Computational Linguistics.

Sennan Liu, Shuang Zeng, and Sujian Li. 2020. Evaluating text coherence at sentence and paragraph levels. In *Proceedings of the 12th Language Resources and Evaluation Conference*, pages 1695–1703.

Yinhan Liu, Myle Ott, Naman Goyal, Jingfei Du, Mandar Joshi, Danqi Chen, Omer Levy, Mike Lewis, Luke Zettlemoyer, and Veselin Stoyanov. 2019. Roberta: A robustly optimized bert pretraining approach. *arXiv preprint arXiv:1907.11692*.

Nikola Ljubešić, Darja Fišer, and Anita Peti-Stantić. 2018. Predicting concreteness and imageability of words within and across languages via word embeddings. In *Proceedings of The Third Workshop on Representation Learning for NLP*, pages 217–222, Melbourne, Australia. Association for Computational Linguistics.

Zhiyi Luo, Yuchen Sha, Kenny Q Zhu, Seung-won Hwang, and Zhongyuan Wang. 2016. Commonsense causal reasoning between short texts. In *Fifteenth International Conference on the Principles of Knowledge Representation and Reasoning*.

Christopher D Manning, Mihai Surdeanu, John Bauer, Jenny Rose Finkel, Steven Bethard, and David McClosky. 2014. The stanford corenlp natural language processing toolkit. In *Proceedings of 52nd annual meeting of the association for computational linguistics: system demonstrations*, pages 55–60.

Peng Qi, Yuhao Zhang, Yuhui Zhang, Jason Bolton, and Christopher D Manning. 2020. Stanza: A python natural language processing toolkit for many human languages. *arXiv preprint arXiv:2003.07082*.

Nils Reimers and Iryna Gurevych. 2019. Sentence-bert: Sentence embeddings using siamese bert-networks. In *Proceedings of the 2019 Conference on Empirical Methods in Natural Language Processing*. Association for Computational Linguistics.

Valerie F Reyna. 2008. A theory of medical decision making and health: fuzzy trace theory. *Medical decision making*, 28(6):850–865.

Valerie F Reyna. 2012. A new intuitionism: Meaning, memory, and development in fuzzy-trace theory. *Judgment and Decision making*.

Valerie F Reyna. 2021. A scientific theory of gist communication and misinformation resistance, with implications for health, education, and policy. *Proceedings of the National Academy of Sciences*, 118(15):e1912441117.

Michael Wilson. 1988. Mrc psycholinguistic database: Machine-usable dictionary, version 2.00. *Behavior research methods, instruments, & computers*, 20(1):6–10.

Christopher R Wolfe, Mitchell Dandignac, and Valerie F Reyna. 2019. A theoretically motivated method for automatically evaluating texts for gist inferences. *Behavior research methods*, 51(6):2419–2437.

Christopher R Wolfe, Mitchell Dandignac, Cynthia Wang, and Savannah R Lowe. 2021. Gist inference scores predict cloze comprehension "in your own words" for native, not esl readers. *Health Communication*, pages 1–8.

Heroes, Villains, and Victims, and GPT-3
Automated Extraction of Character Roles Without Training Data

Dominik Stammbach
ETH Zurich
dominsta@ethz.ch

Maria Antoniak
Cornell University
maa343@cornell.edu

Elliott Ash
ETH Zurich
ashe@ethz.ch

Abstract

This paper shows how to use large-scale pre-trained language models to extract character roles from narrative texts without domain-specific training data. Queried with a zero-shot question-answering prompt, GPT-3 can identify the *hero*, *villain*, and *victim* in diverse domains: newspaper articles, movie plot summaries, and political speeches.

1 Introduction

What makes a good story? According to some leading theories of narrative (e.g. Propp, 1968), a good story has at least three ingredients: a *hero*, a *villain*, and a *victim*. In a classic recipe, the hero defeats the villain to gain justice for the victim. The cohesiveness of these character roles extends even beyond fiction, with social-science research showing the effectiveness of the hero-villain-victim framework in explaining what motivates consumer behavior and political processes (Jones and McBeth, 2010; Clément et al., 2017; Bergstrand and Jasper, 2018).

Motivated by the relevance of narratives to culture and society, a literature in natural language processing (NLP) has arisen to automatically detect characters in texts and annotate their character roles (Bamman et al., 2013a; Jahan and Finlayson, 2019; Piper et al., 2021). In particular, prior work has used dictionary methods to identify heroes, villains, and victims in texts (Gomez-Zara et al., 2018). The previous methods have mixed results, motivating the present research.

This paper explores the use of large pre-trained language models for the task of character role labeling. Operationalizing the problem as a Machine Reading Comprehension Task (MRCP), we provide an input document and ask the language model who is the hero (or villain or victim). As illustrated by the prompt in Figure 1, we directly ask "Who is the hero" (or villain or victim). Thus, we can extract character roles from plain-text documents without in-domain training data.

Who is the villain in the following text?

Text: In questioning the use of hydraulic fracturing in New York to help produce natural gas, you do not note that the technology has been employed and continuously improved for more than 50 years and that studies by the Environmental Protection Agency and the Ground Water Protection Council have not identified a single instance of groundwater contamination. Wells where fracturing is used are specially constructed to protect drinking water sources. Regulatory oversight is extensive. The fluids mostly water that are forced into a well to create pressure to fracture rock are pushed back out by the oil and gas flowing upward for safe processing. Protecting our water supplies is important, as are reductions in greenhouse gas emissions through use of clean-burning natural gas. Banning hydraulic fracturing would be unwarranted and shortsighted, preventing production of large amounts of natural gas that could directly benefit New York consumers for decades and create thousands of good jobs.

Villain: **The villain in this text is the person who is questioning the use of hydraulic fracturing in New York.**

- -

Hero: **The hero in this text is the person who wrote it, who is trying to convince the reader that hydraulic fracturing is a safe and effective way to produce natural gas**
Victim: **The New York consumers**

Figure 1: Zero-Shot Example of the NFP using GPT-3. Prompt in italics, GPT-3 completion in bold (Analogous results for the hero and victim below the dashed line)

We find that a large pre-trained language model, GPT-3 (Brown et al., 2020), is more effective in labeling these character roles than previous methods, across a diverse set of narrative domains. First, we investigate our method on a labeled corpus of newspaper articles about fracking where the three roles—hero, villain, victim—are manually annotated. In that dataset, our language-model approach is over twice as accurate as an existing baseline using a dictionary approach. Second, as an example of possible memorization during pre-training, we report the annotations produced on a selection of Disney movie plot summaries. These results comport well with subjective judgment.

In our third experiment, we apply the method to a corpus of U.S. State of the Union Addresses, 2001-2018. Matching up the character role annotations with the party affiliation of the president, we explore partisan differences in the framing of heroes, victims, and villains. To make this process feasible, we explore clustering of the GPT-3

Proceedings of the 3rd Wordplay: When Language Meets Games Workshop (Wordplay 2022), pages 47 - 56

output, which produces more legible sets of character assignments. These results demonstrate the promise of the method for empirical research in social science and the digital humanities.

These results are of broad interest given the narrative centrality of character archetypes (Propp, 1968). They are of more specific interest in the literature analyzing narrative framing in news media and policy discourse (Jones and McBeth, 2010; Blair and McCormack, 2016). A robust and efficient computational method to extract character roles in text without training data opens up a wide array of research questions to quantitative analysis.

2 Related Work

This paper adds to the work in NLP on automated extraction of character roles from natural language accounts, and in particular the identification of heroes, villains, and victims. The closest paper is Gomez-Zara et al. (2018), who similarly focus on the detection of heroes, villains, and victims in news articles and provide a dictionary-based approach which we will use as a baseline.

On the broader problem of extracting stereotypical character roles, prior work has explored a variety of methods, including the detection of personas using annotated data combined with feature engineering and regression (Bamman et al., 2013b); parsing and lexical matching tools to identify a consistent set of personas (e.g. doctor, nurse, doula) across testimonials about childbirth and then assess the relative power dynamics (Antoniak et al., 2019); annotations of German news and social media sentences for villains and rogues and transformer models to machine-tag these roles (Klenner et al., 2021); clustering of structural plot information from folktales (Jahan et al., 2021); and a combination of NER and clustered phrase embeddings to identify repeatedly occurring entities, along with semantic role labeling to identify how entities are connected by actions (Ash et al., 2021). Our method does not rely on labeled data, but we employ some of these techniques (e.g., clustering) to support the legibility of our results.

The second related literature is treating role extraction as a machine reading comprehension (MRCP) task, which for example has been proposed for semantic role labeling (He et al., 2015). Most related to our work, Liu et al. (2020) and Du and Cardie (2020) interpret event extraction as an MRPC task and leverage pre-trained language models to extract events, producing state-of-the-art results in event extraction and leading us to apply this method for detection of character roles.

In principle, any NLP task can be framed as MRCP or question answering (QA) tasks (see e.g. Kumar et al., 2016; McCann et al., 2018). Interpreting tasks (such as event extraction) as question answering enables us to leverage zero-shot capabilities of pre-trained models. Moreover, these methods are not necessarily dependant on domain-specific features, but solely on plain text. Given the zero-shot capabilities of MRCP tasks across domains (Brown et al., 2020), it is more likely that this procedure transfers across domains.

Our proposed task has many similarities with the computational identification of *framing* (Card et al., 2015) and *agenda setting* (Tsur et al., 2015; Field et al., 2018), as well as with automated *bias measurement* (Bolukbasi et al., 2016; Caliskan et al., 2017). These various tasks all seek to identify the author's written perspective; the same topic can be portrayed differently by different authors, just as the hero or victim might be assigned differently by different authors (Bergstrand and Jasper, 2018). Our identification of the hero, villain, and victim provides yet another method to describe the particular viewpoint expressed in a particular text and to draw comparisons between these various viewpoints over large datasets.

3 Methods

3.1 Labeling Character Roles

Our approach is to frame the labeling of narrative character roles as a machine reading comprehension or closed question answering task. We use auto-regressive language models, i.e., we provide the question and context as prompts to a pre-trained model and decode the answer span token-by-token. We use GPT-3 (Brown et al., 2020), which has proven proficiency in various question-answering tasks (e.g. Rajpurkar et al., 2018). This method allows us to directly leverage knowledge acquired in pre-training on vast amounts of text.

Figure 1 shows an example prompt. We directly ask, "Who is the villain [or hero or victim] in the following text?". That question is followed by the story text, and then the respective character role is repeated to nudge the model to generate the most likely completion of this prompt. We use the same prompt across all experiments in this study, only varying the story text. We use the 175B-parameter davinci model with default decoding parameters.[1]

To benchmark our new model's performance, we consider as a baseline the dictionary-based model from Gomez-Zara et al. (2018). First, they use named entity recognition (NER) to extract important entities from news articles. Second, for each entity, they use the surrounding text and its sentiment polarity and dictionary matching to decide whether an entity is a hero, villain, or victim.[2]

3.2 Corpora

We apply our labeling approach to three corpora, described here. These corpora span three domains and types of narratives: descriptions of current events, fictional stories, and political speeches.

Newspaper Articles. The first domain is newspaper articles. We use a corpus of 66 newspaper articles about fracking published in the *Boulder Daily Camera*, a local Colorado newspaper, from the years 2008-2013. Blair and McCormack (2016) hand-code the three character roles (hero, villain, victim) in these articles.[3] The average length of each article is 682 words.

Disney Movie Plots. The second domain is Disney Movie plots. We selected eleven Disney movies based on a "most well-known classics" list (see Table 2 below). We then downloaded the plot summary section for these movies from Wikipedia. The average plot summary length is 670 words.

U.S. Presidential Speeches. Our third corpus includes presidential speeches given at the annual U.S. State of the Union Address, for the years 2001 to 2018.[4] We split each speech into paragraphs and skip paragraphs containing fewer than 20 words. The final corpus contains $N = 1,379$ paragraphs. Each paragraph contains on average 73 words.

4 Results

This section presents the results, with the three empirical domains reported in turn.

Character	Accuracy GPT-3	Accuracy Baseline	N
Hero	50%	15%	20
Victim	90%	65%	20
Villain	47%	18%	17
All	63%	33%	57

Table 1: Main Evaluation Results: Accuracy of GPT-3 for extracting heroes, villains and victims from The Boulder Daily Camera articles, compared to a dictionary-based baseline descried in (Gomez-Zara et al., 2018). In the last column *N*, we show the number of annotations for each character type present in the data.

4.1 Newspaper Articles about Fracking

Our first analysis applies our GPT-3 method to the collection of news articles about fracking from Blair and McCormack (2016). That paper uses the manual annotations of character roles to analyze framing differences between liberal and conservative media. Regardless of the political leaning, the media outlets in that study framed the public as the victim and the oil and gas industry as the villain. However, the role of hero differed: the liberal media outlet often presented environmental organizations as the hero, while this role is instantiated by specific actors of the oil and gas industry in the conservative outlet.

To automate the annotation process, we use the prompt shown in Figure 1 for each article, the difference being that the text now is the article in question. In the manually annotated data, the authors only find 20 heroes, 20 victims and 17 villains, but our method produces a result for every character role in every article. For evaluation, we only consider model outputs in cases where a true gold annotation exists, and discard all other articles.

In the gold labels from Blair and McCormack (2016), annotations are coarsened such that each specific role (e.g. hero, villain) is mapped to one of a finite set of classes: the public, the government, environmental organizations, or the oil and gas industry. A challenge in the model evaluation is that the language model is not constrained to the finite label set, so the generated text output often does not exactly match the gold labels, even when the output is semantically correct. For the purposes of evaluation, we manually map each GPT-3-generated answer to one of the four categories. The set of GPT-3 outputs and our annotated labels are shown

[1] except for the state-of-the-union address speeches where we use the 13B-parameter curie model for cost reasons.

[2] We could not find the original source code for Gomez-Zara et al. (2018), so we used the implementation available at `https://github.com/meganzhao10/Hero-Villain-Victim`.

[3] Note that the original article also had articles from the *Colorado Springs Gazette*, but we were unable to reproduce that part of the corpus. We contacted the authors to provide the articles, but without success.

[4] These are hosted on Kaggle at `https://www.kaggle.com/datasets/rtatman/state-of-the-union-corpus-1989-2017`.

in Appendix Table 4.

The evaluation results are shown in Table 1. We achieve an overall accuracy of 63%, a large improvement over the dictionary baseline from Gomez-Zara et al. (2018) (33%). While both methods provide decent results for the victims (which is usually assigned to the public), our approach achieves strong gains in detecting the heroes and villains. We observe an almost three-times improvement for both villains and heroes. More detailed metrics (precision, recall, and F1, per annotation type and character role) are reported in Appendix Table 5. To investigate the stability of our method, we replicated the GPT-3 experiment twice. We achieved 65% and 70% overall accuracy in the replication runs.

As an alternative to GPT-3, we also replicate our results with a pre-trained QA model fine-tuned on the union of 8 existing QA datasets (Khashabi et al., 2020).[5] Using the same prompts, we achieve an overall accuracy of 55%, which is not far from GPT-3's performance while using a much smaller model (also having the advantage of being free software). Again, we see the benefits of approaching character role extraction as a QA task leveraging pre-trained models.

4.2 Disney Movie Plot Summaries

Next, we provide qualitative evidence that our method also works in a second domain of popular movie plot summaries. We extract heroes, villains and victims from Wikipedia plot descriptions for widely known Disney movies. Given that these movies contain well-known heroes and villains (if not always victims), it is straight-forward to manually evaluate the quality of the extracted roles. For the same reason, this task also provides some insight into the memorization capabilities of GPT-3, which would have learned about these movies from the training corpus.

The list of annotations for the Disney moves are reported in Table 2. Readers who are familiar with the movies can see that the method works very well in this setting. While some of these annotations are limited or arguable, none are indefensible—there is some reasonable argument for each of these 33 annotations being correct.

As mentioned, these results could be due in part to memorization. We found, for example, that GPT-3 can correctly complete the prompt "Who's the hero in Aladdin?" without the additional narrative text. This memorization seems to be important, because the UnifiedQA model (which would not have a memorization capacity) does make more errors (Appendix Table 6). For example, for *Aladdin*, the model mistakes "Aladdin" for the villain.

4.3 U.S. State of the Union Addresses

In our last application, we show how the method can be used to analyze political discourse in the context of U.S. State of the Union Address speeches, where there is no labeled data, as in the fracking articles, or easily verified set of roles, as in the Disney movies. As we have no ground-truth labels, this section follows a descriptive social-science approach and includes adaptations to our previous methods to improve the legibility of the results.

As before, we apply the method to extract a victim, hero, and villain in each paragraph from the corpus of recent U.S. State of the Union Addresses. The free-form texts generated for the character roles are diverse. We have hundreds of unique answers for each role, with many singletons. To reduce the dimensionality of these outputs and make them more interpretable, we encode the phrases using S-BERT (Reimers and Gurevych, 2019) and apply k-means clustering to the resulting vectors (Jahan et al., 2021; Ash et al., 2021). After manual inspection for different k, we select k=20.

We then use the partisan affiliation of the speakers to score the most Democrat-associated and most Republican-associated clusters in each character role. Formally, we compute the log odds ratio of each cluster w.r.t. the party affiliation of the president giving the speech and show the cluster with the highest and lowest odds ratio.

Table 3 displays the clusters with the highest partisan log odds ratio by character role—that is, the entities taking on this role more often for one or the other party. For Republican presidents (Bush and Trump), the heroes, victims, and villains in SOTU addresses are connected to the U.S. military and wars in the Middle East. Democratic speeches (by Obama) have a more populist flavor, with the average American portrayed as a hero. Intriguingly, for Democrats the villains and victims are both associated with the education system.

[5]We use the unifiedQA-T5-large model found on huggingface.

Movie	Hero	Victim	Villain
101 Dalmatians	Roger Dearly	The Dalmatian Puppies	Cruella de Vil
Aladdin	Aladdin	Aladdin	Jafar
Cinderella	Cinderella	Cinderella	Lady Tremaine
Alice In Wonderland	Alice	Alice	The Queen of Hearts
The Jungle Book	Mowgli	Mowgli	Shere Khan, a man-eating Bengal tiger
Sleeping Beauty	Prince Phillip	Aurora	Maleficent
The Lion King	Simba	Mufasa	Scar
Peter Pan	Peter Pan	Wendy, John, Michael, and the Lost Boys	Captain Hook
Mary Poppins	Mary Poppins	Mr. Banks	Mr. Dawes
The Little Mermaid	Ariel	Ariel	Ursula
Snow White	Snow White	Snow White	The Queen

Table 2: Results for Wikipedia plots of widely known Disney Movies

Role	Democrats	Republicans
Hero	The average family watching tonight, the average person, The average American household, The average person, The average worker, Average American. **Log Odds Ratio: -0.88**	The men and women of the 9/11 generation who have served in Afghanistan and Iraq, The United States military, The military, The veterans, The Cajun Navy volunteers, The man who lost four of his brothers at war, The troops, The troops and civilians who sacrifice every day to protect us, America's veterans . . . **Log Odds Ratio: 1.0**
Victim	The American students, The community colleges, The American student, The person who pays for the good education., The school district, A student, The American public school system, The school, The students who are not American citizens, The students, High school students, The high school graduates in Germany, the American student, The teacher, The school system, Every high school diploma is a ticket to success. **Log Odds Ratio: -1.43**	the coalition to defeat ISIS, ISIS leader, al-Baghdadi, Assad, The UN concluded that Saddam Hussein had biological weapons sufficient to produce over 25,000 liters of anthrax, enough doses to kill several million people, The President of the Iraqi Governing Council, Safia Taleb al-Suhail, Prime Minister Allawi, Iraqi security forces, Iraqi interpreter, Iraqi Government, The Iraqi Government, The American and Iraqi surges have achieved results few of us could have imagined just one year ago. **Log Odds Ratio: 1.42**
Villain	The college, The teacher who comes in early because he knows she might someday cure a disease., The school administration, The educational system, The school in Dillon, South Carolina, The national competition to improve schools is the villain in this text., The school, The Education Secretary, The education reformer, The school system. **Log Odds Ratio: -1.37**	The Taliban, Islamic State, ISIS leader, al-Baghdadi, Intel, The terrorists, The unnamed terrorist group, The terrorist underworld, Al Qaida, International terrorism, Iraqi officials, Iraqi intelligence officers, The enemies of freedom, Radical Islam, Marines, Al Qaeda, Sunni extremists, Syrian occupiers, Radical Shia elements. **Log Odds Ratio: 1.81**

Table 3: Heroes, Victims and Villains extracted from State of the Union speeches. Shown in this table are the entries for the cluster with the highest/lowest odds ratio for Democratic and Republican Presidents

5 Discussion and Future Work

Task formulation. Perhaps the highest-priority limitation of our study is that the method will try to extract a character role from a text, when prompted, even when the role is not present. The newspaper-article evaluation metrics would be much worse if we included the articles missing a role in the test set. In the presidential speeches, in particular, we frequently found that our model assigned the same agent to all three roles—even though villain is mutually exclusive from hero or victim in our evaluation—because there was only one agent mentioned in the speech. There are a number of ways to address this issue. Perhaps the simplest would be to adjust the prompt to allow for a "not applicable" answer, or to ask a preliminary question: "Does this text contain a [role]?" For both of these adjustments, a few-shot approach where the model is provided with some examples could improve performance.

Prompt engineering. Prior work has shown that prompts with subtle differences can product significantly different results (Holtzman et al., 2021; Zhao et al., 2021). Besides few-shot learning, the language-model prompting could also be adjusted to potentially improve performance. Rather than asking about the three roles in three separate prompts, the model could be asked to identify all three simultaneously, for example. The question could be asked in different ways and then the answers aggregated. One could also explore adapting the prompt to constrain the set of entities to a finite set; e.g., in the fracking articles corpus, there was a pre-specified list of four possible entities. Finally, GPT-3 has some decoding hyperparameters that could be tweaked.

Limitations of large language models. Like other NLP models (Bolukbasi et al., 2016), large pre-trained language models can encode harmful human biases (Bender et al., 2021). For example, prior work has shown that narratives generated by

GPT-3 explicitly portray feminine characters as less powerful (Lucy and Bamman, 2021) while also encoding implicit gender biases (Huang et al., 2021). GPT-3 is trained on multiple large datasets, including scraped web text, book texts, and Wikipedia articles. Because of their size, these datasets are difficult to document; even quantifying the number of duplicate documents can be a challenge (Lee et al., 2021) and even more difficult are detailed descriptions, like those called for in data documentation best practices (Gebru et al., 2021). We use GPT-3 to measure authors' framing biases, but it is simultaneously likely that biases encoded in GPT-3 influence our results in ways that are difficult to measure.

Another major limitation to the use of the GPT-3 API is the cost of OpenAI API queries. The queries for our relatively small-scale analysis of state-of-the-union address speeches cost nine dollars using the 13B-parameter GPT-3 model. Scaling this up to larger corpora of thousands or millions of documents, such as the *U.S. Congressional Record* (Ash et al., 2021), would be prohibitively expensive. Hence, using even larger pre-trained models, such as PaLM (Chowdhery et al., 2022), is likely not cost-effective for most academic research. Exploring smaller open-source language models, such as GPT-Neo Black et al. (2021), which can be implemented at scale, is a promising alternative.

Moving beyond pre-trained language models, performance and scalability could be improved through further model training. Fine-tuning GPT-3 for this task is one possibility. A less expensive option would be to use GPT-3 to create a labeled dataset, perhaps with human supervision, for training a smaller student model. That student model could be a distilled autoregressive model or an encoder model like BERT. For MRCP, BERT-like approaches work well for question-answering tasks where the answer is a span of tokens in the input text—in our case, the character being assigned a character role. A limitation of this approach is that character roles are often implicit, rather than explicitly mentioned in the text. BERT-like models work for explicit mentions, but for implicit mentions a generative model like GPT is needed.

Concluding note. In this work, we used the zero-shot capabilities of a large-scale language model to automatically extract heroes, villains and victims from newspaper articles, movie plot summaries, and U.S. presidential speeches. Large pre-trained language models can solve machine reading comprehension tasks for the purposes of labeling short to medium-sized documents, without hand-annotated training data. This approach could be useful for many projects in computational social science and digital humanities.

While promising, our results are still a proof of concept. We have introduced a basic version of the method, which performs better than prior work using a dictionary baseline. But our method's sufficiency for social-science applications is not yet assured, and more work is needed to build up the method and assess its robustness in the field.

References

Maria Antoniak, David Mimno, and Karen Levy. 2019. Narrative paths and negotiation of power in birth stories. *Proceedings of the ACM on Human-Computer Interaction*, 3(CSCW):1–27.

Elliott Ash, Germain Gauthier, and Philine Widmer. 2021. Text semantics capture political and economic narratives.

David Bamman, Brendan O'Connor, and Noah A. Smith. 2013a. Learning latent personas of film characters. In *Proceedings of the 51st Annual Meeting of the Association for Computational Linguistics (Volume 1: Long Papers)*, pages 352–361, Sofia, Bulgaria. Association for Computational Linguistics.

David Bamman, Brendan O'Connor, and Noah A. Smith. 2013b. Learning latent personas of film characters. In *Proceedings of the 51st Annual Meeting of the Association for Computational Linguistics (Volume 1: Long Papers)*, pages 352–361, Sofia, Bulgaria. Association for Computational Linguistics.

Emily M. Bender, Timnit Gebru, Angelina McMillan-Major, and Shmargaret Shmitchell. 2021. On the dangers of stochastic parrots: Can language models be too big? In *Proceedings of the 2021 ACM Conference on Fairness, Accountability, and Transparency*, FAccT '21, page 610–623, New York, NY, USA. Association for Computing Machinery.

Kelly Bergstrand and James M Jasper. 2018. Villains, victims, and heroes in character theory and affect control theory. *Social Psychology Quarterly*, 81(3):228–247.

Sid Black, Leo Gao, Phil Wang, Connor Leahy, and Stella Biderman. 2021. GPT-Neo: Large Scale Autoregressive Language Modeling with Mesh-Tensorflow. If you use this software, please cite it using these metadata.

Benjamin D Blair and Larkin McCormack. 2016. Applying the narrative policy framework to the issues surrounding hydraulic fracturing within the news media: A research note. *Research & Politics*, 3(1):2053168016628334.

Tolga Bolukbasi, Kai-Wei Chang, James Y Zou, Venkatesh Saligrama, and Adam T Kalai. 2016. Man is to computer programmer as woman is to homemaker? debiasing word embeddings. *Advances in neural information processing systems*, 29.

Tom Brown, Benjamin Mann, Nick Ryder, Melanie Subbiah, Jared D Kaplan, Prafulla Dhariwal, Arvind Neelakantan, Pranav Shyam, Girish Sastry, Amanda Askell, Sandhini Agarwal, Ariel Herbert-Voss, Gretchen Krueger, Tom Henighan, Rewon Child, Aditya Ramesh, Daniel Ziegler, Jeffrey Wu, Clemens Winter, Chris Hesse, Mark Chen, Eric Sigler, Mateusz Litwin, Scott Gray, Benjamin Chess, Jack Clark, Christopher Berner, Sam McCandlish, Alec Radford, Ilya Sutskever, and Dario Amodei. 2020. Language models are few-shot learners. In *Advances in Neural Information Processing Systems*, volume 33, pages 1877–1901. Curran Associates, Inc.

Aylin Caliskan, Joanna J Bryson, and Arvind Narayanan. 2017. Semantics derived automatically from language corpora contain human-like biases. *Science*, 356(6334):183–186.

Dallas Card, Amber E. Boydstun, Justin H. Gross, Philip Resnik, and Noah A. Smith. 2015. The media frames corpus: Annotations of frames across issues. In *Proceedings of the 53rd Annual Meeting of the Association for Computational Linguistics and the 7th International Joint Conference on Natural Language Processing (Volume 2: Short Papers)*, pages 438–444, Beijing, China. Association for Computational Linguistics.

Aakanksha Chowdhery, Sharan Narang, Jacob Devlin, Maarten Bosma, Gaurav Mishra, Adam Roberts, Paul Barham, Hyung Won Chung, Charles Sutton, Sebastian Gehrmann, et al. 2022. Palm: Scaling language modeling with pathways. *arXiv preprint arXiv:2204.02311*.

Maéva Clément, Thomas Lindemann, and Eric Sangar. 2017. The "hero-protector narrative": Manufacturing emotional consent for the use of force. *Political psychology*, 38(6):991–1008.

Xinya Du and Claire Cardie. 2020. Event extraction by answering (almost) natural questions. In *Proceedings of the 2020 Conference on Empirical Methods in Natural Language Processing (EMNLP)*, pages 671–683, Online. Association for Computational Linguistics.

Anjalie Field, Doron Kliger, Shuly Wintner, Jennifer Pan, Dan Jurafsky, and Yulia Tsvetkov. 2018. Framing and agenda-setting in Russian news: a computational analysis of intricate political strategies. In *Proceedings of the 2018 Conference on Empirical Methods in Natural Language Processing*, pages 3570–3580, Brussels, Belgium. Association for Computational Linguistics.

Timnit Gebru, Jamie Morgenstern, Briana Vecchione, Jennifer Wortman Vaughan, Hanna Wallach, Hal Daumé III, and Kate Crawford. 2021. Datasheets for datasets. *Commun. ACM*, 64(12):86–92.

Diego Gomez-Zara, Miriam Boon, and Larry Birnbaum. 2018. Who is the hero, the villain, and the victim? detection of roles in news articles using natural language techniques. In *23rd International Conference on Intelligent User Interfaces*, IUI '18, page 311–315, New York, NY, USA. Association for Computing Machinery.

Luheng He, Mike Lewis, and Luke Zettlemoyer. 2015. Question-answer driven semantic role labeling: Using natural language to annotate natural language. In *Proceedings of the 2015 Conference on Empirical Methods in Natural Language Processing*, pages 643–653, Lisbon, Portugal. Association for Computational Linguistics.

Ari Holtzman, Peter West, Vered Shwartz, Yejin Choi, and Luke Zettlemoyer. 2021. Surface form competition: Why the highest probability answer isn't always right. In *Proceedings of the 2021 Conference on Empirical Methods in Natural Language Processing*, pages 7038–7051, Online and Punta Cana, Dominican Republic. Association for Computational Linguistics.

Tenghao Huang, Faeze Brahman, Vered Shwartz, and Snigdha Chaturvedi. 2021. Uncovering implicit gender bias in narratives through commonsense inference. In *Findings of the Association for Computational Linguistics: EMNLP 2021*, pages 3866–3873, Punta Cana, Dominican Republic. Association for Computational Linguistics.

Labiba Jahan and Mark Finlayson. 2019. Character identification refined: A proposal. In *Proceedings of the First Workshop on Narrative Understanding*, pages 12–18, Minneapolis, Minnesota. Association for Computational Linguistics.

Labiba Jahan, Rahul Mittal, and Mark Finlayson. 2021. Inducing stereotypical character roles from plot structure. In *Proceedings of the 2021 Conference on Empirical Methods in Natural Language Processing*, pages 492–497, Online and Punta Cana, Dominican Republic. Association for Computational Linguistics.

Michael D. Jones and Mark K. McBeth. 2010. A narrative policy framework: Clear enough to be wrong? *Policy Studies Journal*, 38(2):329–353.

Daniel Khashabi, Sewon Min, Tushar Khot, Ashish Sabharwal, Oyvind Tafjord, Peter Clark, and Hannaneh Hajishirzi. 2020. UNIFIEDQA: Crossing format boundaries with a single QA system. In *Findings of the Association for Computational Linguistics: EMNLP 2020*, pages 1896–1907, Online. Association for Computational Linguistics.

Manfred Klenner, Anne Göhring, and Sophia Conrad. 2021. Getting hold of villains and other rogues. In

Proceedings of the 23rd Nordic Conference on Computational Linguistics (NoDaLiDa), pages 435–439, Reykjavik, Iceland (Online). Linköping University Electronic Press, Sweden.

Ankit Kumar, Ozan Irsoy, Peter Ondruska, Mohit Iyyer, James Bradbury, Ishaan Gulrajani, Victor Zhong, Romain Paulus, and Richard Socher. 2016. Ask me anything: Dynamic memory networks for natural language processing. In *Proceedings of The 33rd International Conference on Machine Learning*, volume 48 of *Proceedings of Machine Learning Research*, pages 1378–1387, New York, New York, USA. PMLR.

Katherine Lee, Daphne Ippolito, Andrew Nystrom, Chiyuan Zhang, Douglas Eck, Chris Callison-Burch, and Nicholas Carlini. 2021. Deduplicating training data makes language models better. *arXiv preprint arXiv:2107.06499*.

Jian Liu, Yubo Chen, Kang Liu, Wei Bi, and Xiaojiang Liu. 2020. Event extraction as machine reading comprehension. In *Proceedings of the 2020 Conference on Empirical Methods in Natural Language Processing (EMNLP)*, pages 1641–1651, Online. Association for Computational Linguistics.

Li Lucy and David Bamman. 2021. Gender and representation bias in GPT-3 generated stories. In *Proceedings of the Third Workshop on Narrative Understanding*, pages 48–55, Virtual. Association for Computational Linguistics.

Bryan McCann, Nitish Shirish Keskar, Caiming Xiong, and Richard Socher. 2018. The natural language decathlon: Multitask learning as question answering. *arXiv preprint arXiv:1806.08730*.

Andrew Piper, Richard Jean So, and David Bamman. 2021. Narrative theory for computational narrative understanding. In *Proceedings of the 2021 Conference on Empirical Methods in Natural Language Processing*, pages 298–311, Online and Punta Cana, Dominican Republic. Association for Computational Linguistics.

Vladimir Iakovlevich Propp. 1968. *Morphology of the folktale*. University of Texas Press.

Pranav Rajpurkar, Robin Jia, and Percy Liang. 2018. Know what you don't know: Unanswerable questions for SQuAD. In *Proceedings of the 56th Annual Meeting of the Association for Computational Linguistics (Volume 2: Short Papers)*, pages 784–789, Melbourne, Australia. Association for Computational Linguistics.

Nils Reimers and Iryna Gurevych. 2019. Sentence-BERT: Sentence embeddings using Siamese BERT-networks. In *Proceedings of the 2019 Conference on Empirical Methods in Natural Language Processing and the 9th International Joint Conference on Natural Language Processing (EMNLP-IJCNLP)*, pages 3982–3992, Hong Kong, China. Association for Computational Linguistics.

Oren Tsur, Dan Calacci, and David Lazer. 2015. A frame of mind: Using statistical models for detection of framing and agenda setting campaigns. In *Proceedings of the 53rd Annual Meeting of the Association for Computational Linguistics and the 7th International Joint Conference on Natural Language Processing (Volume 1: Long Papers)*, pages 1629–1638, Beijing, China. Association for Computational Linguistics.

Zihao Zhao, Eric Wallace, Shi Feng, Dan Klein, and Sameer Singh. 2021. Calibrate before use: Improving few-shot performance of language models. In *Proceedings of the 38th International Conference on Machine Learning, ICML 2021, 18-24 July 2021, Virtual Event*, volume 139 of *Proceedings of Machine Learning Research*, pages 12697–12706. PMLR.

Article title	Role	Annotated	GPT-3 answer	Equivalent
No. 3: Gloves come off in the fight over fracking	villain	Oil and gas industry	the oil and gas industry	1
Polis to oil and gas: please stop suing the communities I represent	hero	Fed Govt	Jared Polis	1
Anti-fracking measures win in Lafayette, Boulder, Fort Collins	victim	General or specific public	Lafayette	1
Anti-fracking measures win in Lafayette, Boulder, Fort Collins	villain	Oil and gas industry	the oil and gas industry	1
Colorado Oil and Gas Aaaociation gives $600K to fight fracking bans on Front Range Ballots	hero	Oil and gas industry	Merrily Mazza	0
Colorado Oil and Gas Aaaociation gives $600K to fight fracking bans on Front Range Ballots	victim	General or specific public	Lafayette Campaign for Energy Choice	1
Colorado Oil and Gas Aaaociation gives $600K to fight fracking bans on Front Range Ballots	villain	Environmental Orgs	The Colorado Oil and Gas Association	0
Lafayette to draft resolutions of opposition to fracking ban, utility occupation tax	victim	General or specific public	Lafayette	1
Broomfield approves agreement with oil and gas operator	hero	Enviromnental Orgs	The City Council	0
Broomfield approves agreement with oil and gas operator	victim	General or specific public	Anthem residents	1
Broomfield approves agreement with oil and gas operator	villain	Local Govt	Sovereign	0
Ballot initiative to ban fracking in Lafayette garners enough signiatures to move forward	victim	General or specific public	Lafayette	1
Extension of Boulder County fracking moratorium deemed a win for many	victim	General or specific public	the citizens of Boulder County	1
Lafayette anti-fracking effort draws canvassers	hero	Enviromnental Orgs	Cliff Willmeng	1
Lafayette anti-fracking effort draws canvassers	victim	Oil and gas industry	Lafayette	0
Lafayette anti-fracking effort draws canvassers	villain	Enviromnental Orgs	East Boulder County United	1
Broomfield unlikely to pursue fracking moratorium	hero	Enviromnental Orgs	The City Council	0
Broomfield unlikely to pursue fracking moratorium	victim	General or specific public	the community in Broomfield	1
Broomfield unlikely to pursue fracking moratorium	villain	Oil and gas industry	The City Council	0
Boulder County Commissioner Elise Jhones to debate Gov John Hickenlooper on fracking	hero	Local Govt	Boulder County Commissioner Elise Jones	1
Boulder County Commissioner Elise Jhones to debate Gov John Hickenlooper on fracking	victim	General or specific public	Boulder County Commissioner Elise Jones	0
Boulder County Commissioner Elise Jhones to debate Gov John Hickenlooper on fracking	villain	State Govt	Elise Jones	1
Anti-fracking group to present Lafayette with petition for ban	hero	Enviromnental Orgs	Anti-fracking group	1
Anti-fracking group to present Lafayette with petition for ban	victim	General or specific public	Lafayette	1
Anti-fracking group to present Lafayette with petition for ban	villain	Oil and gas industry	East Boulder County United	0
Lafayette to pursue moratorium on new oil and gas permits	hero	Oil and gas industry	Lafayette	0
Group urges ban on fracking Activists ask Lafayette for moratorium	hero	Enviromnental Orgs	John Chinnery	0
Group urges ban on fracking Activists ask Lafayette for moratorium	victim	General or specific public	the community of Lafayette	1
Group urges ban on fracking Activists ask Lafayette for moratorium	villain	Enviromnental Orgs	John Chinnery	0
In Erie, oil and gas companies to pay twice as much for water	hero	Enviromnental Orgs	The town last week doubled its commercial water rate . . .	0
In Erie, oil and gas companies to pay twice as much for water	victim	General or specific public	The town of Erie	1
In Erie, oil and gas companies to pay twice as much for water	villain	Oil and gas industry	The oil and gas companies	1
Anti-fracking group to provide air-monitoring equiptment to erie residents	hero	General or specific public	The anti-fracking group Erie Rising.	0
Anti-fracking group to provide air-monitoring equiptment to erie residents	hero	Enviromnental Orgs	The anti-fracking group Erie Rising.	1
Anti-fracking groups to protest Encanas drilling operation near Erie schools Saturday	hero	Enviromnental Orgs	Anti-fracking groups	1
Anti-fracking groups to protest Encanas drilling operation near Erie schools Saturday	victim	General or specific public	Erie schools	1
Anti-fracking groups to protest Encanas drilling operation near Erie schools Saturday	villain	Oil and gas industry	Encana	1
Erie mothers, children descend on Encana headquarters with anti-fracking petition	victim	General or specific public	Erie mothers and children	1
Dirty air in Erie linked to gas drilling	hero	Enviromnental Orgs	The researcher with the National Oceanic and Atmospheric Administration	0
Dirty air in Erie linked to gas drilling	victim	General or specific public	Erie residents	1
Dirty air in Erie linked to gas drilling	villain	Oil and gas industry	Industry	1
Lawsuit from COGA brings Lafayette into thick of fight over oil and gas drilling	hero	Fed Govt	Lafayette	0
Pro-fracking group alleges 'systemic failures' in Broomfield election	hero	Enviromnental Orgs	BJ Nikkel	1
Colorado Oil and Gas Association gives $600K to fight fracking bans on Front Range ballots	victim	General or specific public	Lafayette campaign for energy choice	1
Voter frustration fills ballot with citizen initiatives in Boulder, Broomfield counties	hero	General or specific public	A frustrated voter	1
Voter frustration fills ballot with citizen initiatives in Boulder, Broomfield counties	villain	Other	-	0
Broomfield tightening requirements for oil and gas companies	villain	Oil and gas industry	The City Council	0
Coming off win at Boulder County level, anti-frackers turn focus statewide	hero	Enviromnental Orgs	Anti-frackers	1
In talk at CU-Boulder, Hickenlooper says he is 'constantly attacked now for being in the pocket of oil and gas'	hero	Oil and gas industry	Governor John Hickenlooper	0
Broomfield postpones hearing on North Park fracking application	hero	Enviromnental Orgs	Jackie Houle	1
Broomfield postpones hearing on North Park fracking application	victim	General or specific public	Concerned residents of Broomfield	1
'Bucket Brigade': Anti-fracking citizen effort to monitor the air in Erie	victim	General or specific public	Erie residents	1
'Bucket Brigade': Anti-fracking citizen effort to monitor the air in Erie	villain	Oil and gas industry	Global Community Monitor	0
Hundreds gather to protest Encana Corp.'s fracking operation in Erie	victim	General or specific public	The community	1
Hundreds gather to protest Encana Corp.'s fracking operation in Erie	villain	Oil and gas industry	Encana Corp.	1
Erie eyes agreements with oil and gas operators	villain	Oil and gas industry	Erie	0
Fracking discussion packs Erie Town Hall, no action taken on moratorium	victim	General or specific public	The community of Erie	1

Table 4: Article title, annotated label from (Blair and McCormack, 2016), the GPT-3 output, and the author's determination whether the generated output is equivalent to the manual annotation.

Role	Entity	Pr	Rc	F1	N
Hero	Enviromnental Orgs	0.88	0.58	0.70	12
	(local, State or Fed) Government	0.50	1.00	0.67	3
	Oil and gas industry	0.00	0.00	0.00	3
	Other	0.00	0.00	0.0	0
	General or specific public	0.20	0.50	0.29	2
Villain	Enviromnental Orgs	0.50	0.33	0.40	3
	(local, State or Fed) Government	0.33	0.50	0.40	2
	Oil and gas industry	0.86	0.55	0.67	11
	Other	0.50	1.00	0.67	1
	General or specific public	0.00	0.00	0.00	0
Victim	Enviromnental Orgs	0.00	0.00	0.00	0
	(local, State or Fed) Government	0.00	0.00	0.00	0
	Oil and gas industry	0.00	0.00	0.00	1
	General or specific public	0.94	0.89	0.92	19

Table 5: Detailed precision, recall and F1 scores for the different annotation types and roles. N denotes the number of annotated examples in the data, e.g. the data contains 12 Environmental Orgs as heroes.

Movie	Hero	Victim	Villain
101 Dalmations	Roger Dearly	Anita	Cruella de Vil
Aladdin	Aladdin	Aladdin	Aladdin
Cinderella	the hero is Cinderella.	Lucifer	Lucifer
Alice In Wonderland	Alice	the Queen of Hearts	the Queen of Hearts
The Jungle Book	Mowgli	Shere Khan	Shere Khan
Sleeping Beauty	Phillip	Prince Phillip	Maleficent
Lion King	Simba	Scar	Scar
Peter Pan	Peter Pan	Peter Pan	Hook
Mary Poppins	Mary Poppins	the bank	banker
The Little Mermaid	Ariel	Ariel	Ursula
Snow White	the dwarfs	the queen	the queen

Table 6: Results for Wikipedia plots of widely known Disney Movies using the unifiedqa-t5-large model, a T5 model fine-tuned on 8 existing QA datasets.

Narrative Detection and Feature Analysis in Online Health Communities

Achyutarama R. Ganti and **Steven R. Wilson** and **Zexin Ma**
Oakland University
{ganti,stevenwilson,zexinma}@oakland.edu

Xinyan Zhao
University of North Carolina
ezhao@unc.edu

Rong Ma
Butler University
rma@butler.edu

Abstract

Narratives have been shown to be an effective way to communicate health risks and promote health behavior change, and given the growing amount of health information being shared on social media, it is crucial to study health-related narratives in social media. However, expert identification of a large number of narrative texts is a time consuming process, and larger scale studies on the use of narratives may be enabled through automatic text classification approaches. Prior work has demonstrated that automatic narrative detection is possible, but modern deep learning approaches have not been used for this task in the domain of online health communities. Therefore, in this paper, we explore the use of deep learning methods to automatically classify the presence of narratives in social media posts, finding that they outperform previously proposed approaches. We also find that in many cases, these models generalize well across posts from different health organizations. Finally, in order to better understand the increase in performance achieved by deep learning models, we use feature analysis techniques to explore the features that most contribute to narrative detection for posts in online health communities.

1 Introduction

Narrative forms of communication are widely used for conveying information and building connections. Broadly defined as a representation of someone's experience of a series of events (Bilandzic and Busselle, 2013), narratives take on different formats, ranging from short anecdotes and testimonials to lengthy entertainment TV shows and movies (Kreuter et al., 2007).

In the health context, extensive research has found that narratives are more effective than non-narratives (e.g., statistics, didactic arguments) in communicating health risks (Janssen et al., 2013; Ma, 2021) and promoting health behavior change (Kreuter et al., 2010). Moreover, telling personal illness narratives helps patients to better cope with the illness (Carlick and Biley, 2004) and for health care professionals to better understand the illness (Kalitzkus and Matthiessen, 2009). Given that social media has become a widely used platform for cancer patients and their caregivers to share stories and connect with others (Gage-Bouchard et al., 2017; Hale et al., 2020), it is critical to understand what cancer narratives are told on social media and how they engage social media users.

However, in order to understand the impact of narratives in online communication, narratives must first be *identified* in social media datasets. Doing this often requires annotations from subject matter experts, which can be a costly process and difficult to scale up to massive datasets. In this work, we seek to understand the extent to whether natural language processing methods, specifically, fine-tuned large language models, can be used to automatically detect narratives within social media posts in the health domain using only a relatively small number of expert annotations. Additionally, analyzing models that are able to successfully detect narratives can provide *insights* into the types of textual features that are most related to narrative text within a corpus.

Toward these aims, we collect and annotate a dataset of social media posts created by breast cancer organizations and address the following research questions:

RQ1 Which text classification models provide the best performance for automatic narrative detection for social media texts posted by breast cancer organizations?

RQ2 How does the ability to detect narratives generalize across posts written by different organizations?

RQ3 Which features are most important for automatic narrative detection in this context?

Proceedings of the 3rd Wordplay: When Language Meets Games Workshop (Wordplay 2022), pages 57 - 65

To answer **RQ1**, We compare a range of text classification methods and find that transformer-based deep-learning based methods outperform classical approaches like support vector machines, as well as the previous state-of-the-art method for detecting narratives within health-related social media posts (Dirkson et al., 2019). To answer **RQ2**, we split our dataset so that the same organizations' accounts are not used for both train and test data, finding that in most cases, it is possible for our best models to generalize well across organizations. Finally, to answer **RQ3**, we use machine learning analysis tools to identify which features contribute most to the prediction of narratives, finding that references to people, such as pronouns and names, as well as state-of-being verbs like "is", contributed strongly to cases where models predicted that texts contained narratives.

Our results suggest that automatic detection of narratives in social media posts is a promising application of text classification, and can help ease the burden of manual annotation for researchers seeking to study the relationship between narrative and other variables of interest at scale.[1]

2 Related Work

Online health communities have been computationally studied before in order to understand how users show social support for one another (Andy et al., 2021), to automatically extract information needs of patients (Romberg et al., 2020), and to identify linguistic patterns associated with anxiety (Rey-Villamizar et al., 2016). Additionally, Antoniak et al. (2019) analyzed birth stories from an online forum and demonstrated the utility of these stories for computational work. Machine learning models have been trained using textual health forum data to predict attributes such as the sentiment (Ali et al., 2013) or cancer stage of the patients posting to forums (Jha and Elhadad, 2010). Yet, most work in the area of computational analysis of online medical forums has not considered the importance of narrative. At the same time, computational approaches incorporating and extracting narratives have led to advances in the study of corporate finance (Zmandar et al., 2021), environmental issues (Armbrust et al., 2020), the analysis of clinical records (Jung et al., 2011), and emotion classification within stories (Tanabe et al., 2020).

[1]Code and annotations are publicly available at `https://github.com/ou-nlp/NarativeDetection`.

As NLP datasets, narratives are often directly collected by sampling data from sources that are already known to use narrative based on the genre of the corpus, such as literary works (Hammond et al., 2013), doctors' notes (Elhadad et al., 2015), or fan fiction (Yoder et al., 2021). In the social media domain, data is often sampled in a way to ensure the presence of narratives, e.g., by collecting posts from specific subreddits which typically contain narrative style posts (Yan et al., 2019).

In other cases, the presence or location of narrative content is unknown beforehand and needs to be to detected or extracted. This might be done using filtering criteria like the length of the post or the presence of predefined linguistic patterns (Vijayaraghavan and Roy, 2021). However, some datasets contain a balanced mixture of both narrative and non-narrative content, and quick rule-based filtering is not adequate. In the domain of online health communities specifically, prior work has relied on expert annotations to determine what should or should not be considered a narrative (Dirkson et al., 2019; Verberne et al., 2019). In each of these works, text classification models were trained to automatically determine whether or not a given post contained narratives, and support vector machines (SVM) using bag-of-words or character n-gram features were found to be the best approach.

We build upon this existing work by applying deep learning text classification models to the task of narrative detection in social media posts from breast cancer organizations as an example use case that includes personal narratives, texts for which narrative presence is unknown *a priori*, and provide the potential for enabling larger scale studies of the importance of narratives in health communication. We find that these approaches outperform SVM-based models similar to those used by Dirkson et al. (2019)[2] and Verberne et al. (2019) and explore their effectiveness on our dataset throughout the rest of this paper.

3 Data Collection and Annotation

A list of breast cancer non-profit organizations was identified from the Canadian cancer survivor net-

[2]We contacted the authors of these papers but they could not share their data due to user privacy restrictions. Therefore, we only use the same approach reported by the authors, rather than applying our proposed deep learning models on the same datasets that were used in those studies.

Organization	Posts	Tokens	Narrative
Susan G. Komen	212	10845	65.57%
NBCF USA	144	11433	58.33%
Breast Cancer Now	186	18932	64.52%
AFWBC Canada	116	7636	21.55%
NBCF Australia	191	11161	25.13%
Total	**849**	**60007**	**49.0%**

Table 1: Annotated data set statistics.

work partners page[3]. We selected five organizations with the most Facebook followers and spanning several different countries, including Susan G. Komen For the Cure, National Breast Cancer Foundation USA, the UK-based Breast Cancer Now, A Future Without Breast Cancer (Canadian Cancer Society), and the National Breast Cancer Foundation Australia. Their Facebook posts and engagement metrics from 2016 to 2021 were downloaded using CrowdTangle[4] ($N = 8,580$).

The top 10% posts in terms of total interactions were sampled for annotation. Following standard procedures in content analysis (Riff et al., 2014), two expert coders annotated the presence of narratives (48.83%). All disagreements were resolved by discussion, and the consensus results were used for further analyses (i.e., the highest standard of intercoder reliability) (Krippendorff, 2004). The overall agreement rate was above 0.9. For this study, we omit 9 posts which did not contain any text and only videos or images. The breakdown of the annotated dataset by non-profit organization account is presented in Table 1.

4 Detecting Narrative Style

Next, we set out to determine how well various text classification models could detect the presence of narratives given the expert annotations as training data. For this experiment, we appended data from all five non-profit organizations into a single dataset. All the data points were then shuffled and split using 80% of the data for training, and each 10% for validation and test sets. The metrics that were used for model evaluation are the F1 scores, Precision, and Recall of the narrative class. We consider two categories of models: classical machine learning models using bag-of-words features, and transformer-based deep learning models.

For the **classical models**, we experiment with various preprocessing schemes in terms of lowercasing, lemmatization, and stopword removal, and choose the approach that gave the best performance on our validation set. That process included: lowercasing, removing URLs, lemmatization using NLTK's wordnet (Miller, 1995) lemmatizer, and stopword removal using the NLTK (Bird et al., 2009). However, given the importance of pronouns in narrative detection as evidenced in prior work (Dirkson et al., 2019), we do not remove pronouns as part of our stopword removal step. The models that we consider are Naive Bayes, Logistic Regression, and SVM-classification, using each model's scikit-learn (Pedregosa et al., 2011) Python implementation. Model-specific hyperparameters were also tuned using the validation set as described in Appendix A.

Additionally, we consider the best reported approach from Dirkson et al. (2019), which is the previous best reported narrative detection model for online health forum data. We use the code provided by the authors to both preprocess the data and train the predictive model. The authors used an SVM classifier with a linear kernel and character-level trigram features as input, and so we refer to this model as SVM-trigram in our results.

For the **deep learning models**, we use DistilBERT (Sanh et al., 2019), BERT (Devlin et al., 2019), and RoBERTa (Liu et al., 2019) models based on the `DistilBERT-Base-Uncased`, `BERT-Base-Uncased`, and `RoBERTa-Base` checkpoints available from HuggingFace (Wolf et al., 2019). The tokenizer for each model was automatically determined using the `AutoTokenizer()` class. We use the output representation of the `[CLS]` token as input to the classification layer (the default approach when using the HuggingFace `Trainer` class). Hyperparameters are described in Appendix A.

The results of running each of these models are presented in Table 2. It is evident that deep learning models are capable of distinguishing narratives from non-narratives in the sequences, with BERT showing the best overall performance. Among the classical machine learning methods, the SVM model outperformed others with an F1 score and accuracy of 0.901. Although our classical methods didn't perform poorly, there is a substantial gain in F1-score when using the deep learning approaches. Therefore, for the generalization experiments in the next section, we only consider the best performing model, i.e., the BERT model.

[3]`https://survivornet.ca/connect/partners`

[4]`https://www.crowdtangle.com/`

Model	F1	Prec	Recall
Baseline-narrative	0.680	**1.000**	0.512
Naive Bayes	0.879	0.952	0.816
SVM	0.901	0.928	0.876
Log. Regr.	0.891	0.880	0.902
SVM-trigram	0.889	0.935	0.847
DistilBERT	0.964	**1.000**	0.931
BERT	**0.988**	0.977	**1.000**
RoBERTa	0.977	**1.000**	0.956

Table 2: Narrative class F1, Precision, and Recall scores of the text classification models on the narrative detection task, separated into groups of classical ML and deep learning methods. The score of the performing model(s) for each metric is listed in **bold**. SVM-trigram is the best performing model from (Dirkson et al., 2019). Baseline-narrative is the score achieved by labeling all texts as narrative.

Target	F1	Prec	Recall
Susan G. Komen	0.949	0.973	0.927
Breast Cancer Now	**0.991**	0.903	**1.000**
NBCF Australia	0.900	0.903	0.979
NBCF USA	0.976	0.976	0.976
AFWBC Canada	0.936	**1.000**	0.880

Table 3: Generalization performance using the best classifier (BERT) by training on all accounts except for the target account, and testing on the target account.

Train	F1	Prec	Recall
Susan G. Komen	0.917	0.852	**0.993**
Breast Cancer Now	0.777	0.979	0.645
NBCF Australia	**0.953**	0.961	0.945
NBCF USA	0.877	0.791	0.985
AFWBC Canada	0.914	**0.976**	0.859

Table 4: Generalization performance using the best classifier (BERT) by training on one account and testing on the remaining four target accounts.

4.1 Generalizing across accounts

A model's ability to generalize to unseen data is key to a successful deployment. Our deep learning[5] models can successfully classify the presence of narratives in social-media posts, but it is possible that they overfit to features that are specific to the set of organizations that generated the posts included in our dataset. To evaluate the generalizability of the BERT model to data from unseen organizations, we re-trained the model on data from only four organizations, leaving the fifth one out as test data. We then repeat this process again for each of the five organizations, so that each organization is used as the held-out test set once, and as part of the training set in all other cases.

The results of this experiment are presented in Table 3. The posts from the organization Breast Cancer Now held out as test data were the easiest to generalize to (F1 score of 0.991) compared to the other combinations. On the other hand, the model slightly under-performed when trained on data from all organizations leaving NBCF Australia as test set with a F1 score of 0.900. However, in all cases, this shows that there is good potential for models trained on a subset of organizations to generalize well to others.

We then performed one slightly varied version of the same experiment to further determine model generalizability. Here, we chose a dataset from only one organization as the training set, and used the remaining four datasets as testing data. As before, we repeat this experiment five times, using each organization as training data once, and testing in all other cases. This experiment helps to determine the potential for cross-organization transfer when we have very limited data or data from a single source. Given the very small amount of data for some of the organizations, we found that the size of the training set was too small to learn effective models in some cases. Therefore, we chose to up-sample our training set by 200%, (duplicating each training instance) which we found empirically to give better results in the low training data case. From the final result (Table 4), we observe that the model trained on NBCF Australia performs the best overall, achieving an F1 score that is within a few points of the model trained on data from all organizations from Table 2. On the other hand, the model trained only on Breast Cancer Now posts had poor generalization performance on the data from the other organizations, suggesting that having data from only a single organization is not always enough to guarantee good generalizability.

5 Analysis of Narrative Detection Models

We have established that deep learning models are very effective at detecting narratives from social media data, substantially outperforming classical machine learning approaches. However, it is not immediately apparent *why* these models are able to achieve better F1 scores. Therefore, in this section, we use model interpretability tools to further examine which features contributed to the ability of our models to detect narratives.

We chose the best performing models in each cat-

[5]We also experimented with our best performing classical ML model, SVM, in the same way, but the results were not as strong (Appendix B).

latasha is feeling victorious over her breast cancer diagnosis after ringing the bell on her last treatment day! join us in wishing her well on her survivorship journey.

(a) Post 1: BERT predicts "narrative" (correct).

latasha is feeling victorious over her breast cancer diagnosis after ringing the bell on her last treatment day! join us in wishing her well on her survivorship journey.

(b) Post 1: SVM predicts "narrative" (correct).

breast cancer has changed the lives of thousands of people every year. people like nadia, sharon, kimberley and anjum. learn more about their personal and unique experiences as these 4 breast cancer survivors open up to help raise awareness and support others on a similar journey.

(c) Post 2: BERT predicts "narrative" (correct).

breast cancer has changed the lives of thousands of people every year. people like nadia, sharon, kimberley and anjum. learn more about their personal and unique experiences as these 4 breast cancer survivors open up to help raise awareness and support others on a similar journey.

(d) Post 2: SVM predicts "non-narrative" (incorrect).

fatigue is a common side effect of breast cancer treatment, but many people don't realise they're not the only one experiencing it. it's different to just feeling tired. discover tips for managing cancer-related fatigue in becca, our app that helps you adapt to life beyond treatment

(e) Post 3: BERT predicts "non-narrative" (correct).

fatigue is a common side effect of breast cancer treatment, but many people don't realise they're not the only one experiencing it. it's different to just feeling tired. discover tips for managing cancer-related fatigue in becca, our app that helps you adapt to life beyond treatment

(f) Post 3: SVM predicts "narrative" (incorrect).

Figure 1: Feature importance visualization for three posts, one per row, that were classified by our top-performing deep learning model (BERT) and classical machine learning model (SVM). Orange (blue) shading indicates the token was found to be important for the "narrative" ("non-narrative") class by LIME, with the color intensity indicating the degree of importance. Post 1 was correctly classified by both models, while posts 2 and 3 were correctly classified by BERT but incorrectly classified by the SVM model.

egory, i.e., BERT for the deep learning approaches, and SVM for the classical models, and use the explainable AI tool for Local Interpretable Model Agnostic Explanation (LIME; Ribeiro et al. (2016)) to understand the significance of text-based features to each model. In both cases, we use the LIME explainer function[6] to learn which features best explain the narrative class and non-narrative class. We chose 5000 samples and 25 features as parameters for the function, based on the suggested default values and our desire to include a reasonable number of features per example.

Each instance in the test dataset is examined using LIME, which generates an importance score for each feature (token) in the input based on how much it contributes to predictions for the positive class (narrative) or negative class (non-narrative). For a given feature j in a given text i, a higher positive score W_{ij} denotes greater importance of that feature in the overall narrative class and a lower positive score denotes a weaker importance of that feature for the same class. Likewise, a greater negative value W_{ij} for a feature indicates a stronger association with predictions of the non-narrative class. Several examples of LIME explanations are presented in Figure 1. We can see that for posts where both models made the correct prediction, the set of important features is approximately the same. However, when BERT made the correct prediction and SVM did not, we notice that BERT places a greater emphasis on first names in the case of narratives, and features like "fatigue" and "common", which refer side effects of breast cancer, are correctly identified as important indicators that the post does not contain a narrative.

While these qualitative results are highly useful, LIME only provides the W_{ij} score for a specific text, i, yet we sought to quantitatively understand which features were important across the entire test set. Therefore, we use Global Aggregations of Local Explanations (GALE; van der Linden et al. (2019)) to aggregate the LIME scores. For the purposes of aggregation, we set a cut-off of $\epsilon = 0.001$ and consider any $W_{ij} < \epsilon$ as a score of 0. A feature importance score of zero indicates that the feature does not explain much of either the narrative or the non-narrative class while making predictions. GALE suggests several different methods for aggregating scores, but we use the Global Average Importance I^{AVG} as it was found to correlate well with external measures of feature importance for model classification. The Global Average Importance I_j^{AVG} for a given feature j is defined as:

$$I_j^{AVG} = \frac{\sum_{i=1}^{N} |W_{ij}|}{\sum_{i:W_{ij} \neq 0} \mathbb{1}}$$

where N is the number of texts in the corpus.

Table 5 shows the top and bottom 10 aggregated feature importance scores for both BERT and SVM. Both the models put more emphasis on pronouns and first names as they are more personal to the storyteller or subject of the narrative. Our feature analysis results align with that of Dirkson et al. (2019) who noted that narratives in health forums are characterized by health related words and first

[6]From `https://github.com/marcotcr/lime`

BERT		*SVM*	
word	**score**	**word**	**score**
celeste	0.29	her	0.22
she	0.28	taylor	0.20
latasha	0.24	my	0.19
beautiful	0.17	she	0.18
mother	0.16	app	0.15
her	0.15	peace	0.14
barbe	0.14	becca	0.13
hall	0.11	tip	0.13
found	0.09	rest	0.12
is	0.09	his	0.11
s	-0.04	face	-0.10
don'	-0.04	study	-0.11
significant	-0.04	run	-0.11
round	-0.05	mammogram	-0.11
myresearchstory	-0.05	mel	-0.12
awareness	-0.05	addy	-0.15
free	-0.06	steph	-0.15
it	-0.06	listen	-0.16
"	-0.06	mondaymotivation	-0.17
increase	-0.08	song	-0.19

Table 5: Top and bottom ten aggregated feature importance scores for BERT (left side) and SVM (right side) models trained for narrative detection. Larger positive values indicate a greater overall importance for the "narrative" class, while more negative values were more important for predicting the "non-narrative" class.

BERT – SVM	
word	**score**
celeste	0.29
latasha	0.24
barbe	0.14
mother	0.12
hall	0.11
beautiful	0.11
she	0.10
found	0.09
is	0.09
i	0.08
strong	-0.02
diagnosis	-0.02
bell	-0.03
reality	-0.03
be	-0.05
journey	-0.06
her	-0.07
it	-0.08
his	-0.09
my	-0.12

Table 6: Top and bottom ten features that differed in importance the most between the BERT and SVM model. Scores with a larger value had more overall importance for the BERT model, while features with a smaller value had more importance for the SVM model.

person pronouns. Also, since breast cancer is more common among women, it is more common to see feminine pronouns and first names related to women with the only exception being the token "his" which can be found as an important feature for the "narrative" class in the SVM model. Upon further inspection, we found that there are instances referring to women as "his wife" and "his mother" which further validates the model's choice for the token in the positive list. We also note verbs such as "found" (connected to "lump", which also had a positive score for both models but is not in the top ten for either) and "is".

Considering the tokens with negative values, indicating that they were more relevant when predicting the "non-narrative class", we found words related to scientific studies, sharing songs, and describing clinical procedures. Hashtags such as "myreserachstory" and "mondaymotivation" were also present, indicating posts that may have been trying to seek engagement through means other than the use of narrative. While Our BERT model was successful in detecting narratives by learning associations between features like pronouns and first names, the SVM model failed to consistently learn these associations as indicated by the placement of several first names in the non-narrative (negative valued) end of the list.

While these results illustrate which features were important to each model, they do not directly *quantify* the difference between the BERT and SVM. To investigate that further, we checked the extent to which the degree of importance I_j^{AVG} for each feature differed between BERT and the SVM model (Table 6). For each feature in the list obtained from SVM, we subtract the corresponding aggregated importance score from BERT for that feature. If the result is positive, it indicates that the BERT model puts more emphasis on that feature, whereas if the result is negative, it indicates that SVM gives more importance for that feature compared to BERT model for predicting the "narrative" class. We observe that BERT assigns a higher weight for first names and the pronoun "she" has a higher importance for BERT compared to SVM whereas, the pronoun "her" appears to be given greater importance by the SVM model compared to BERT.

6 Conclusion

In this paper, we show that deep learning models like BERT, DistilBERT and RoBERTa are effective at detecting narratives from social media data. Previous research focused on the use of classical machine learning models to understand narratives in online health discussion forums, but we demonstrate that deep learning models outperform these when detecting the presence of narratives. We studied generalizability of the deep learning models across organizations, finding that overall, models are able to generalize well across accounts, suggesting that deep learning models provided with sufficient data can perform well on an unseen dataset with similar distributions. We also analyze the performance of deep learning models with explainable AI methods, uncovering important features that contribute to narratives in a particular context.

However, there are certain limitations and challenges associated with these models. Although they are quite successful at understanding narratives, performance of deep learning models is directly proportional to the quality of the dataset and they are highly susceptible to annotator and dataset bias.

With the growing amount of health information being shared on social media, understanding narratives becomes extremely important to study public health behavior and estimate health risks. The work described in this paper is a step towards helping researchers automatically annotate narratives in social media posts, thus enabling larger scale studies of the impact of narratives on health conversations.

References

Tanveer Ali, David Schramm, Marina Sokolova, and Diana Inkpen. 2013. Can I hear you? sentiment analysis on medical forums. In *Proceedings of the Sixth International Joint Conference on Natural Language Processing*, pages 667–673, Nagoya, Japan. Asian Federation of Natural Language Processing.

Anietie Andy, Brian Chu, Ramie Fathy, Barrington Bennett, Daniel Stokes, and Sharath Chandra Guntuku. 2021. Understanding social support expressed in a COVID-19 online forum. In *Proceedings of the 12th International Workshop on Health Text Mining and Information Analysis*, pages 19–27, online. Association for Computational Linguistics.

Maria Antoniak, David Mimno, and Karen Levy. 2019. Narrative paths and negotiation of power in birth stories. *Proc. ACM Hum.-Comput. Interact.*, 3(CSCW).

Felix Armbrust, Henry Schäfer, and Roman Klinger. 2020. A computational analysis of financial and environmental narratives within financial reports and its value for investors. In *Proceedings of the 1st Joint Workshop on Financial Narrative Processing and MultiLing Financial Summarisation*, pages 181–194, Barcelona, Spain (Online). COLING.

Helena Bilandzic and Rick Busselle. 2013. Narrative persuasion. *The Sage handbook of persuasion: Developments in theory and practice*, 2:200–219.

Steven Bird, Ewan Klein, and Edward Loper. 2009. *Natural language processing with Python: analyzing text with the natural language toolkit.* " O'Reilly Media, Inc.".

Alice Carlick and Francis C Biley. 2004. Thoughts on the therapeutic use of narrative in the promotion of coping in cancer care. *European Journal of Cancer Care*, 13(4):308–317.

Jacob Devlin, Ming-Wei Chang, Kenton Lee, and Kristina Toutanova. 2019. BERT: Pre-training of deep bidirectional transformers for language understanding. In *Proceedings of the 2019 Conference of the North American Chapter of the Association for Computational Linguistics: Human Language Technologies, Volume 1 (Long and Short Papers)*, pages 4171–4186, Minneapolis, Minnesota. Association for Computational Linguistics.

AR Dirkson, Suzan Verberne, Wessel Kraaij, AM Jorge, R Campos, A Jatowt, and S Bhatia. 2019. Narrative detection in online patient communities. In *Proceedings of Text2Story—Second Workshop on Narrative Extraction From Texts co-located with 41th European Conference on Information Retrieval (ECIR 2019)*, pages 21–28. CEUR-WS.

Noémie Elhadad, Sameer Pradhan, Sharon Gorman, Suresh Manandhar, Wendy Chapman, and Guergana Savova. 2015. SemEval-2015 task 14: Analysis of clinical text. In *Proceedings of the 9th International Workshop on Semantic Evaluation (SemEval 2015)*, pages 303–310, Denver, Colorado. Association for Computational Linguistics.

Elizabeth A Gage-Bouchard, Susan LaValley, Michelle Mollica, and Lynda Kwon Beaupin. 2017. Cancer communication on social media: examining how cancer caregivers use facebook for cancer-related communication. *Cancer nursing*, 40(4):332–338.

Brent J Hale, Ryan Collins, and Danielle K Kilgo. 2020. Posting about cancer: Predicting social support in imgur comments. *Social Media+ Society*, 6(4):2056305120965209.

Adam Hammond, Julian Brooke, and Graeme Hirst. 2013. A tale of two cultures: Bringing literary analysis and computational linguistics together. In *Proceedings of the Workshop on Computational Linguistics for Literature*, pages 1–8, Atlanta, Georgia. Association for Computational Linguistics.

Eva Janssen, Liesbeth van Osch, Hein de Vries, and Lilian Lechner. 2013. The influence of narrative risk communication on feelings of cancer risk. *British Journal of Health Psychology*, 18(2):407–419.

Mukund Jha and Noémie Elhadad. 2010. Cancer stage prediction based on patient online discourse. In *Proceedings of the 2010 Workshop on Biomedical Natural Language Processing*, pages 64–71, Uppsala, Sweden. Association for Computational Linguistics.

Hyuckchul Jung, James Allen, Nate Blaylock, William de Beaumont, Lucian Galescu, and Mary Swift. 2011. Building timelines from narrative clinical records: Initial results based-on deep natural language understanding. In *Proceedings of BioNLP 2011 Workshop*, pages 146–154, Portland, Oregon, USA. Association for Computational Linguistics.

Vera Kalitzkus and Peter F Matthiessen. 2009. Narrative-based medicine: potential, pitfalls, and practice. *The Permanente Journal*, 13(1):80.

Matthew W Kreuter, Melanie C Green, Joseph N Cappella, Michael D Slater, Meg E Wise, Doug Storey, Eddie M Clark, Daniel J O'Keefe, Deborah O Erwin, Kathleen Holmes, et al. 2007. Narrative communication in cancer prevention and control: a framework to guide research and application. *Annals of behavioral medicine*, 33(3):221–235.

Matthew W Kreuter, Kathleen Holmes, Kassandra Alcaraz, Bindu Kalesan, Suchitra Rath, Melissa Richert, Amy McQueen, Nikki Caito, Lou Robinson, and Eddie M Clark. 2010. Comparing narrative and informational videos to increase mammography in low-income african american women. *Patient education and counseling*, 81:S6–S14.

Klaus Krippendorff. 2004. *Content analysis: An introduction to its methodology*. Sage publications.

Yinhan Liu, Myle Ott, Naman Goyal, Jingfei Du, Mandar Joshi, Danqi Chen, Omer Levy, Mike Lewis, Luke Zettlemoyer, and Veselin Stoyanov. 2019. Roberta: A robustly optimized bert pretraining approach. *arXiv preprint arXiv:1907.11692*.

Zexin Ma. 2021. The role of narrative pictorial warning labels in communicating alcohol-related cancer risks. *Health Communication*, pages 1–9.

George A Miller. 1995. Wordnet: a lexical database for english. *Communications of the ACM*, 38(11):39–41.

F. Pedregosa, G. Varoquaux, A. Gramfort, V. Michel, B. Thirion, O. Grisel, M. Blondel, P. Prettenhofer, R. Weiss, V. Dubourg, J. Vanderplas, A. Passos, D. Cournapeau, M. Brucher, M. Perrot, and E. Duchesnay. 2011. Scikit-learn: Machine learning in Python. *Journal of Machine Learning Research*, 12:2825–2830.

Nicolas Rey-Villamizar, Prasha Shrestha, Farig Sadeque, Steven Bethard, Ted Pedersen, Arjun Mukherjee, and Thamar Solorio. 2016. Analysis of anxious word usage on online health forums. In *Proceedings of the Seventh International Workshop on Health Text Mining and Information Analysis*, pages 37–42, Auxtin, TX. Association for Computational Linguistics.

Marco Tulio Ribeiro, Sameer Singh, and Carlos Guestrin. 2016. " why should i trust you?" explaining the predictions of any classifier. In *Proceedings of the 22nd ACM SIGKDD international conference on knowledge discovery and data mining*, pages 1135–1144.

Daniel Riff, Stephen Lacy, and Frederick Fico. 2014. *Analyzing media messages: Using quantitative content analysis in research*. Routledge.

Julia Romberg, Jan Dyczmons, Sandra Olivia Borgmann, Jana Sommer, Markus Vomhof, Cecilia Brunoni, Ismael Bruck-Ramisch, Luis Enders, Andrea Icks, and Stefan Conrad. 2020. Annotating patient information needs in online diabetes forums. In *Proceedings of the Fifth Social Media Mining for Health Applications Workshop & Shared Task*, pages 19–26, Barcelona, Spain (Online). Association for Computational Linguistics.

Victor Sanh, Lysandre Debut, Julien Chaumond, and Thomas Wolf. 2019. Distilbert, a distilled version of bert: smaller, faster, cheaper and lighter. *arXiv preprint arXiv:1910.01108*.

Hikari Tanabe, Tetsuji Ogawa, Tetsunori Kobayashi, and Yoshihiko Hayashi. 2020. Exploiting narrative context and a priori knowledge of categories in textual emotion classification. In *Proceedings of the 28th International Conference on Computational Linguistics*, pages 5535–5540, Barcelona, Spain (Online). International Committee on Computational Linguistics.

Ilse van der Linden, Hinda Haned, and Evangelos Kanoulas. 2019. Global aggregations of local explanations for black box models. *CoRR*, abs/1907.03039.

Suzan Verberne, Anika Batenburg, Remco Sanders, Mies van Eenbergen, Enny Das, Mattijs S Lambooij, et al. 2019. Analyzing empowerment processes among cancer patients in an online community: A text mining approach. *JMIR cancer*, 5(1):e9887.

Prashanth Vijayaraghavan and Deb Roy. 2021. Modeling human motives and emotions from personal narratives using external knowledge and entity tracking. In *Proceedings of the Web Conference 2021*, pages 529–540.

Thomas Wolf, Lysandre Debut, Victor Sanh, Julien Chaumond, Clement Delangue, Anthony Moi, Pierric Cistac, Tim Rault, Rémi Louf, Morgan Funtowicz, Joe Davison, Sam Shleifer, Patrick von Platen, Clara Ma, Yacine Jernite, Julien Plu, Canwen Xu, Teven Le Scao, Sylvain Gugger, Mariama Drame, Quentin Lhoest, and Alexander M. Rush. 2019. Huggingface's transformers: State-of-the-art natural language processing.

Xinru Yan, Aakanksha Naik, Yohan Jo, and Carolyn Rose. 2019. Using functional schemas to understand social media narratives. In *Proceedings of the Second Workshop on Storytelling*, pages 22–33, Florence, Italy. Association for Computational Linguistics.

Michael Yoder, Sopan Khosla, Qinlan Shen, Aakanksha Naik, Huiming Jin, Hariharan Muralidharan, and Carolyn Rosé. 2021. FanfictionNLP: A text processing pipeline for fanfiction. In *Proceedings of the Third*

Workshop on Narrative Understanding, pages 13–23, Virtual. Association for Computational Linguistics.

Nadhem Zmandar, Mahmoud El-Haj, Paul Rayson, Ahmed Abura'Ed, Marina Litvak, Geroge Giannakopoulos, and Nikiforos Pittaras. 2021. The financial narrative summarisation shared task FNS 2021. In *Proceedings of the 3rd Financial Narrative Processing Workshop*, pages 120–125, Lancaster, United Kingdom. Association for Computational Linguistics.

A Model Hyperparameters

For Naive Bayes, we did not tune any hyperparameters. For the SVM classifier, we considered linear, polynomial, and rbf kernels, and found the polynomial kernel to work the best. We set the regularization parameter $C = 2$. For the Logistic Regression classifier, we tried various values for the regularization parameter C in the range of $\{0.01, 0.1, 0.2, 1, 2, 10\}$ and found that $C = 1$ gave the best results. For the deep learning models, we use a batch size of 16 with a weight decay of 0.01 and a learning rate of 2e-5, training for 5 epochs.

B Generalizability of SVM model

We performed the same experiments from section 4.1 using an SVM model (the best performing classical model from our experiments in section 4). The results are presented in Tables 7 and 8.

Target	F1	Prec	Recall
Susan G. Komen	0.884	0.776	0.972
Breast Cancer Now	**0.901**	0.883	0.921
NBCF Australia	0.830	**0.970**	0.730
NBCF USA	0.851	0.952	0.769
AFWBC Canada	0.830	0.710	**1.000**

Table 7: Generalization performance using the best classical ML model (SVM) by training on all accounts except for the target account, and testing on the target account.

Train	F1	Prec	Recall
Susan G. Komen	0.803	0.946	0.697
Breast Cancer Now	**0.824**	0.886	0.770
NBCF Australia	0.730	0.582	0.981
NBCF USA	0.733	**0.965**	0.591
AFWBC Canada	0.457	0.296	**1.000**

Table 8: Generalization performance using the best classical ML model (SVM) by training on one account and testing on the remaining four target accounts.

Looking from the Inside: How Children Render Character's Perspectives in Freely Told Fantasy Stories

Max van Duijn[1] and **Bram van Dijk**[1] and **Marco Spruit**[1,2]
[1]Leiden Institute of Advanced Computer Science
[2]Leiden University Medical Centre
{m.j.van.duijn,b.m.a.van.dijk,m.r.spruit}
@liacs.leidenuniv.nl

Abstract

Story characters not only perform actions, they typically also perceive, feel, think, and communicate. Here we are interested in how children render *characters' perspectives* when freely telling a fantasy story. Drawing on a sample of 150 narratives elicited from Dutch children aged 4-12, we provide an inventory of 750 instances of character-perspective representation (CPR), distinguishing fourteen different types. Firstly, we observe that character perspectives are ubiquitous in freely told children's stories and take more varied forms than traditional frameworks can accommodate. Secondly, we discuss variation in the use of different types of CPR across age groups, finding that character perspectives are being fleshed out in more advanced and diverse ways as children grow older. Thirdly, we explore whether such variation can be meaningfully linked to automatically extracted linguistic features, thereby probing the potential for using automated tools from NLP to extract and classify character perspectives in children's stories.

1 Introduction

Story characters are everywhere around us: we meet them in the books we read, the TV series we get caught up in, or in a gossipy tale we tell each other during everyday social gatherings. Some characters may be modelled on real people, whereas others exist only in the imagined worlds of fantasy and fiction. In its most basic form, a story character is an entity involved in some kind of action or description. Yet typically we also get to share in some of its *perspectives* on the storyworld and the objects, events, and other characters within it. There are long-standing traditions in linguistics and literary studies, especially within the subfields of sylistics and narratology, studying the ways in which such character perspectives can be rendered (e.g. Banfield, 1973; Leech and Short, 2007; Vandelanotte, 2009). Three main patterns commonly distinguished in studies of 'Speech and Thought Representation' are *direct*, *indirect*, and *free-indirect speech* or *thought* (see Section 3 for examples). While most attention has been paid to literary texts, scholars have also identified such patterns in cinema (Verstraten, 2009), theatre (McConachie and Hart, 2006), and other domains such as news articles (Sanders, 2010), everyday conversations between parents and young infants (Köder, 2016), or speech from patients with psycho-pathological conditions (van Schuppen et al., 2020).

It is largely an open question as of yet how children render characters' intentions, perceptions, emotions, speech, and thought when asked to freely tell a fantasy story. This is worthwhile exploring for a variety of reasons. It has been widely argued that representing different perspectives reflects a central function of language usage (e.g. Dancygier et al., 2016): human interaction is characterised by 'polyphony', meaning that we rarely only express our own perspective. Instead, the default is that we use language to *orchestrate* multiple perspectives. Even though this pervades all speech domains, stories are a key finding place for linguistic and narratological patterns supporting this function (Fludernik, 1996), and arguably also the 'sandbox' where both children and adults test and refine their perspective-orchestration skills (Vermeule, 2009). Mapping how children of different ages render character perspectives is as such of interest to anguage acquisition research, but also to cognitive psychology as it provides insight into how children learn to understand the social world and others' minds, and the role narratives can play herein. Tools from Natural Language Processing (NLP) can fuel all such research, for example by automatically identifying contextual information associated with different character perspectives. NLP researchers, in turn, can learn about phenomena relevant for embarking on tasks involving more complex classification or extraction of perspectivised content.

Proceedings of the 3rd Wordplay: When Language Meets Games Workshop (Wordplay 2022), pages 66 - 76
July 15, 2022

In the current contribution we draw on a sample of 150 stories, told by children aged 4-12 as part of storytelling workshops we offered across The Netherlands. Our sample features 750 instances of character-perspective representation (CPR), which we categorise in fourteen different types based on manual qualitative analysis. As discussed below, the type categories and analytical framework we adopt are primarily inspired on 'classic' STR literature (mainly Leech and Short, 2007). However, we complement our framework with additional types based on research into children's development as storytellers and relevant insights from cognitive linguistics, allowing for a more refined and inclusive way of mapping character perspectives.

The best way to introduce our approach in concrete terms is to discuss the analysis of an example story. Doing so will also make clear how we position this paper: as an effort to build a bridge between *qualitative* analysis of narrative material as traditionally done in the Humanities, and *quantitative* analysis, driven by the automatic extraction of linguistic information, as customary in computational approaches. In 2.1-2.4 below we first provide more details on our corpus, sample, and annotations. In 2.5 we introduce two automatically extracted linguistic variables, lexical and syntactic complexity, and in 2.6 our aims and hypotheses are formulated. Section 3 opens with the discussion of the example story, followed by an inventory of all instances of CPR we have identified in our sample, classified in fourteen types. We explore how the occurrence of different types of perspective representation varies with the age of the storytellers in 4.1, and with lexical and syntactic characteristics of the utterances in which they occur in 4.2.

2 Background and Methods

2.1 Children's Stories and Our Corpus

Children tell stories to themselves and others as part of their daily play activities (Sutton-Smith, 1986; Cremin et al., 2017). While being the source of a lot of fun in the first place, such storytelling has been analysed as a form of *cognitive play* that is essential for child development in various key areas, including the acquisition and refinement of communicative skills (Southwood and Russell, 2004), organising knowledge of the (social) world (McKeough and Genereux, 2003), and empathising with others and understanding their motives and intentions (Gallagher and Hutto, 2008; Nicolopoulou, 2018; Zunshine, 2019). Phenomena of CPR are situated at a natural crossroads of these key developmental areas: their absence or presence in freely told stories arguably reflects children's communicative abilities, but also their understanding of the social world and capacity to imagine others' inner workings. Here we do explore the occurrence of different patterns of character representation across different age groups, and we believe that our contribution can ultimately fuel research in developmental psychology and language acquisition research. However, it is important to note that claims about whether the patterns we find in our stories are indicative of a specific child's development are outside the scope of this paper.

The storytelling workshops for the creation of our database were held between 2019-2021 at seven elementary schools, a daycare, and a community centre located in various areas across in The Netherlands. Each session was held in a classroom setting involving 5-30 children at a time, of varying ages between 4-12 (see 2.2 for details). Sessions started by discussing some general characteristics of stories (e.g. "Where can you find stories?", "What kind of stories do you like?") and interactively narrating an exemplary fantasy story with the participating children. Next, we invited children to take the floor and tell a fantasy story about a topic free of choice. After informing children about this, voice recordings were made, which were pseudonymised and transcribed afterwards by the authors and research assistants Transcripts were double-checked for consistency with the audio files. As of now, we have over 600 stories in our database called ChiSCor (Children's Story Corpus).[1] Our data collection and data management protocols were assessed and approved by the Ethics Review Committee of Leiden University's Faculty of Science (file no. 2020 – 002).

2.2 Sample

For the current research we drew a sample from our database according to the following steps:

- We included only the first story told by each child (many children told multiple stories),

[1]We aim to make ChiSCor available to the research community later this year, after fully completing the annotation process and including additional metadata. The subset of stories used in this paper, along with our current annotations and scripts, are available already via the Open Science Framework (OSF): `https://osf.io/9q32v/?view_only=b80ce5cb0e4c49cabb7697f93f40ab73`

which reduces dependence between stories. This yielded a subset of 350 stories.

- We selected stories with a length (in number of words, $\bar{x} = 108.64, \sigma = 99.62$) falling in the interquartile range (IQR), i.e. 50% around the median ($min = 4, Q1 = 35, Med = 75, Q3 = 151, max = 626$), to prevent over- or under-representation of data from children with exceptionally long or short stories.

- We then defined three age categories, 'Young', 'Middle' and 'Older', in line with the division common in Dutch primary education into 'Onderbouw', 'Middenbouw', and 'Bovenbouw'. 'Young' corresponds to 'Onderbouw' which involves ages 4-6; 'Middle' corresponds to 'Middenbouw' which involves ages 6-9; 'Older' corresponds to 'Bovenbouw' which involves ages 9-12.

- We included 150 stories in total (12879 words), 50 for each group. For the young and middle groups these were randomly drawn out of 60 and 78 stories falling within the IQR, respectively. The older group had only 39 stories within the IQR; here we added 11 stories closest to $Q1$ and $Q3$ to balance groups.

2.3 Annotation Procedure

The 150 stories were put into a large table in random order and without showing additional information to avoid (unconscious) interference with decisions in the annotation process.[2] Existing line breaks, introduced during transcription of the audio recordings according to a standardised protocol, were used to chunk each story into smaller units, henceforth referred to as 'utterances'. We identified 568 unique characters that in total made 1472 appearances (the same character can obviously appear in multiple utterances within the same story), 722 of which involved only descriptions or simple actions without insight being offered into the character's perspective. The remaining 750 appearances were given one of fourteen different labels representing our types of CPR. In rare cases where multiple types applied, the most 'advanced' label was chosen in terms of the stages introduced in 3.

The first author, who has a background in grammar and narratological theory, took the lead in the annotation process, while regularly discussing categorical distinctions as well as individual utterances with the second author. In some specific cases, expertise was gathered from external experts. While we can see how this procedure may be problematic from the perspective of current standards in NLP, two considerations should be added with regards to our approach in this paper. Firstly, we point out that we base our annotations on long-standing traditions of textual analysis within cognitive linguistics, narratology, and stylistics, known to support high degrees of intersubjective agreement and reproducibility between researchers within these fields (for a broader discussion of a 'grounded theory' approach, see Charmaz, 2006). Secondly, it is important to note that the statistical analyses in 4.1 and 4.2 are based on *merged* categories. While discussion is sometimes possible about the most appropriate type label for specific utterances (e.g. deciding between direct and indirect speech on grammatical grounds; see also Köder, 2016), such discussions would rarely affect the overarching merged category under which this utterance falls.[3] Nevertheless, we consider it an important next step within our larger project to gather CPR annotations from at least one additional, independent annotator.

In 3 our full system of fourteen types of CPR is discussed, along with the example story and inventory of the occurrence of each type in our sample.

2.4 Ego-Narration vs. the Rest

It is important to single out one type category beforehand: *ego-narration*. We see this as a 'preliminary stage' of the fuller mastery of CPR that is characteristic of the other thirteen types. We marked cases as *ego-narration* if there was no (or an unclear) distinction between the child narrating the story and a referent indicated with first-person pronouns ('I', 'me', 'we', 'us') within a story. Consider the following example from story with ID 022501 in ChiSCor: '[...] and I do a lot of horse riding / and ride a lot of horses / and we have a lot of very sweet horses in the stables [...]'. This counts as *ego-narration*, since the 'I' who regularly does a lot of horse riding refers to the child in the immediate situation of telling the story. This is different in the following example from story 082601: '[...] and then came well myself in fact who came with a gun / and I said why are you fighting Batman and Superman [...]', since the 'I' is making an

[2] E.g. the age or school of the storyteller. Note that such interference could only be avoided to a certain degree; after all, we were ourselves involved in recording the stories.

[3] An exception is found in line 7 of the example story in 3.

appearance in a story world clearly detached from the here-and-now of telling the story.[4]

The rationale for singling out *ego-narration* as a preliminary phenomenon is that it evidences a lack of 'transcendence' (Zeman, 2020), marking a departure from the actual speaker and their immediate here-and-now, which we consider a key feature of storytelling. Such transcendence is warranted by a distinction between the child telling the story (ego), the narrator seen as a theoretical entity or 'role', and characters within the story.[5] What the remaining thirteen types of character representation have in common is that they exhibit storytelling in this sense, i.e. a specific form of communication in which a narrator-entity provides all kinds of linguistic cues inviting listeners (or readers) to imagine a storyworld including objects, characters, actions, events, etc. (Dancygier, 2011). In this way it is possible for narrators to tell a story entirely from the 'outside perspective', without directly cuing listeners to imagine what the storyworld would look like from any character's point of view; this is what we observed in utterances containing only character appearances consisting of descriptions or simple actions, plus in utterances containing no character appearances at all. In each of the remaining utterances we found essentially a mix of narrator and character perspectives. The way in which, and degree to which, these character perspectives were explicitly fleshed out and/or separated from that of the narrator, determine which of the thirteen types applies.

2.5 Lexical and syntactic complexity

There is evidence that socio-cognitive skills, in particular the capacity to understand and reason about others' mental states known as Theory of Mind (Apperly, 2010), are positively correlated to lexical and syntactic proficiency in children. For example, children possessing a larger vocabulary, or mastering clausal complementation, perform better in reasoning about others' mental states in standardised clinical tasks (for a review see Milligan et al., 2007). As mentioned in Section 2.1 above, we see overlap between children's development of socio-cognitive capacities and their ability to flesh out characters' perspectives in a narrative. Therefore we include lexical and syntactic complexity here as two theoretically motivated features, that can potentially provide us with the linguistic context in which different types of CPR occur, and connect this to age groups of the storytellers in our sample. Doing so, we might also anticipate linguistic information encoded in (the middle layers of deeper) neural networks, that could be helpful for automatically extracting and/or classifying perspectivised information in children's narratives in the future (Jawahar et al., 2019).

To calculate Lexical Complexity (LC) we approximated for each word in utterance U featuring a character perspective, its lemma probability $P(L)$ by its relative frequency count in the BasiScript lexicon, a large benchmark corpus of written child output (Tellings et al., 2018). Lexical perplexity $PP(U)$ is given by $U = L_1, L_2...L_N$ with $PP(U) = \sqrt[N]{\frac{1}{P(L1, L_2, L_3...L_N)}}$. Thus, utterances with more infrequent lemmas show higher perplexity with respect to the lexicon. Lemma frequency has been argued to be a good measure of lemma complexity given that infrequent lemmas are overall harder to learn (Vermeer, 2001). To calculate Syntactic complexity (SC), for each utterance U featuring a character perspective we extracted a dependency tree, a directed graph $G = (V, A)$ with V as the set of words and A as the set of arcs indicating dependency relations between words. We extracted the maximum number of arcs between the root node and a leaf node in U. This measure of syntactic complexity is also known as 'tree depth' and is a common measure of syntactic complexity: utterances employing longer paths are syntactically more complex (Dell'Orletta et al., 2011).

2.6 Aims and Hypotheses

First it is our aim to explore variation in the use of CPR types within our sample as a whole (3). Secondly, we hypothesise that the occurrence of these types is not uniformly distributed over age groups. From the idea that some CPR types can be seen as more advanced than others, as we discuss in 3, we predict that preliminary and basic types of CPR occur more often at younger ages, while intermediate and advanced types are more often found in older children (4.1). Thirdly, we aim to explore links between CPR types and linguistic information extracted using NLP tools. We predict

[4] The full Dutch stories can be found in our OSF repository (fn. 1). Utterances are separated with forward slashes. English translations are our own and were made only for the purpose of discussing them here; annotations within the project are based on the Dutch originals.

[5] We refrain from going into the widely debated narratological concept of the narrator here and refer to Zeman (2020) for a to-the-point overview.

that more advanced types of CPR are more likely to co-occur with utterances exhibiting higher lexical and syntactic complexity (4.2).

3 Types, Inventory, and Staging of CPR

In order to illustrate our approach in more detail, we will now discuss the analysis of a story excerpt, featuring five types of CPR found throughout our sample. Afterwards, the remaining types will be briefly introduced along with a complete overview with examples and counts in Table 1.

1. *a girl went to the zoo and she saw a huge lot of tigers and other animals [...]*
2. *and she went home all alone*
3. *but her little brother was left behind he was sitting on the monkey*
4. *then said the sister of the little boy where is my little brother now*
5. *she went back again to the zoo*
6. *then she saw that the little brother was sitting on the monkey*
7. *oh little brother where are you now*
8. *the end*

First of all, we can observe that this is a story narrated in third person, past tense. For a large part it consists of narrator descriptions of actions and situations ('went to the zoo', utterance 1; 'went home all alone', 2; 'her little brother was left behind' and 'sitting on a monkey', 3; etc.); however, as listeners/readers we also get a few glimpses into the perspective of one character: the 'girl'.

In utterance 1 we learn about the animals she 'saw'. It could be defended that this is still entirely the narrator's voice telling us 'from the outside' what the girl would have been seeing at the zoo. Yet, as discussed in 2.4 above, and in line with what cognitive linguists have argued in recent years (e.g. van Duijn and Verhagen, 2018), we suggest that perspectivisation of content in narratives can be seen on a cline ranging from pure narrator view on the one extreme, to full character view with minimal narrator mediation on the other extreme. Following this approach, the report of what the girl 'saw' in utterance 1 implies a modest but certain invitation for listeners or readers of the story to imagine the girl's perspective on objects within the storyworld: 'a huge lot of tigers and other animals'. This is a case of *character perception* (*PER*) in our system of types. Another instance is found in utterance 6.

What is more, we note a difference between how the situation of the 'little brother' is described ('was left behind', 'sitting on a monkey', utterance 3) and some of the descriptions of actions performed by the 'girl' (e.g. 'went home all alone', utterance 2; 'went back again to the zoo', utterance 5). Following developmental psychologists and children's story researchers Nicolopoulou and Richner (2007) we classify the latter as cases of *intention-in-action* (*IIA*), i.e. actions coupled to a clear goal or result within the immediate story context. Compared to *PER* and other forms of CPR discussed below, *IIA* represents the lowest degree of inviting a shift from the narrator's to a character's perspective. Yet mere descriptions of a character's situation, appearance, attributes, or actions without an immediately specified result or goal do not invite such a shift at all, or to an even lesser degree. This is why we see *IIA* as the most basic type in our staging of perspective representation.

In utterance 4 we find a case of *direct speech* (*DS*) with an inquit formula ('said the sister of the little boy') and a reported clause ('where is my little brother now'[6]). The reported clause has three features supporting our classification as *DS*. Firstly, a shift to the present tense can be observed ('is' as opposed to 'said' in the inquit formula). Secondly, there is a shift from the third to the first person as expressed by the pronoun 'my'. And thirdly, the addition of 'now' ('nou' in the original Dutch story) can be seen as an idiomatic exclamation, expressing a degree of wonder or confusion (which is not satisfactory covered by the English translation 'now'). This wonder or confusion is clearly to be interpreted as part of the 'girl'-character's experience, and not of the narrator's, just as 'my little brother' from the character's point of view indicates the same referent as 'the little boy' from the narrator's point of view. The present tense is congruent with the girl-character's experience at the moment of speaking within the story plot.

Finally, utterance 7 features *free direct speech* (*FDS*). Here we see the same shift to present tense ('are') and the same exclamation ('nou' in the Dutch original), complemented with another exclamation at the beginning of the sentence ('oh'). The absence of an inquit formula makes it a case of *FDS* rather than *DS*. Or, a different possible interpretation of utterance 7 is that we are looking at a form of 'monologue intérieur' in which the girl-character produces this utterance for herself,

[6]The absence of a question mark after the reported clause is due to standardised transcription of the recorded oral stories.

Type	Example & Story ID	Counts
ego-narration (EGO-NARR)	'i love music' (061401)	47
intention-in-action (IIA)	'she went back again to the zoo' (072201)	350
character perception (PER)	'she saw a huge lot of tigers and other animals' (072201)	53
NRSA	'she did not ask the teacher about it' (033401)	15
direct speech (DS)	'then said the sister [...] where is my little brother now' (072201)	74
free direct speech (FDS)	'oh little brother where are you now' (072201)	14
indirect speech (IS)	'she said that they had to stop swimming' (114201)	5
free indirect speech (FIS)	n.a.	-
NRMS	'he did not like that' (061401)	98
viewpoint package (VP)	'because he entered secretly' (101901)	44
direct thought (DT)	'then he thought I want to protect her' (052901)	17
free direct thought (FDT)	'shall I make some invitations for her friends' (052901)	1
indirect thought (IT)	'the family thought that they were safe' (112301)	17
free indirect thought (FIT)	'he could wish for everything that he now wants' (014901)	15

Table 1: Our fourteen types of CPR with examples, story IDs (see fn. 1), and counts of occurrence in our sample. *NRSA* and *NRMS* refer to *narrative report of speech act* and *narrative report of mental state*. *FIS* was not found.

rendering it a case of *free direct thought* rather than *speech*. The context does not resolve this ambiguity. One can argue that she is addressing the boy, given that she has just found him in the preceding utterance, but one can equally well argue that utterance 7 should be read as an internal expression of her surprise, given that he is sitting on a monkey.

In Table 1 it can be seen that *ego-narration* (*EGO-NARR*), the preliminary stage of CPR we distinguished in 2.4, occurs 47 times in our sample. *IIA*, which we consider to be CPR in its most basic form, is with 350 occurrences by far the most frequently observed type. Usage of *IIA* entails that the narrator reports what a character is doing, and to what end. Similarly, with *PER*, of which we recorded 53 instances, it is the narrator who reports what a character is perceiving. Both happen without the narrator intruding into the character's mental world: rather, a description is given that invites the listener to imagine what a character intends or perceives, thereby effectively getting to share in the character's perspective on the storyworld to some degree. *Narrative reports of speech acts* (*NRSA*) and cases of *(free) indirect speech* (*(F)IS*), relate what a character says or said primarily in the words of the narrator, while *(free) direct speech* (*(F)DS*) is to be taken as the literal rendition of a character's words. Still, what all these forms of speech reporting have in common is that they do not imply that the narrator has direct insight into characters' minds. Here too it is strictly speaking the listener who is cued to draw conclusions about a character's perspective based on the report of what they say or said. This contrasts with thought representation in its different forms, where access to a character's mind is relied on by default.[7] This goes for *direct thought* (*DT*) and *indirect thought* (*IT*) alike, even though in the latter case the contents of the character's thoughts are rendered in the narrator's words (see also the examples in Table 1). *Narrative Report of Mental State* (*NRMS*) is an ambiguous type in this respect; it can sometimes imply access to a character's mind, but in other cases reflect the narrator's reading of a mental state 'from the outside' (viz. characterising someone as 'happy' can be based on their behaviour as well as on narratorial access to their inner life).

Looking at frequencies in the representation of speech and thought, it is apparent that *DS* is the most used type of speech representation (74 occurrences), whereas the much more indirect *NRMS* is most frequent (98) in representing thought. Finally, the type *Viewpoint Package* (*VP*), recorded 44 times, is introduced by us based on recent work (van Duijn and Verhagen, 2018) that we found useful in our children's story context. In short, *Viewpoint Packages* are single words implying a mental state contrasting with a state of affairs or with another mental state. For example, if a character does something 'secretly', this implies that there is a perspective from which this is *not noticed* and a perspective from it is indeed *desired* that it remains unnoticed.

We follow Nicolopoulou and Richner (2007) in their analysis suggesting that, for a storyteller, *IIA* and *PER* require less advanced efforts on a cognitive level, compared to handling character speech

[7]In classic narrative theory this is referred to as narrator omniscience; cf. Margolin (2014). Furthermore, for an extensive discussion of *FIS* and *FIT* as forms mixing elements of direct and indirect representation, see Vandelanotte (2009).

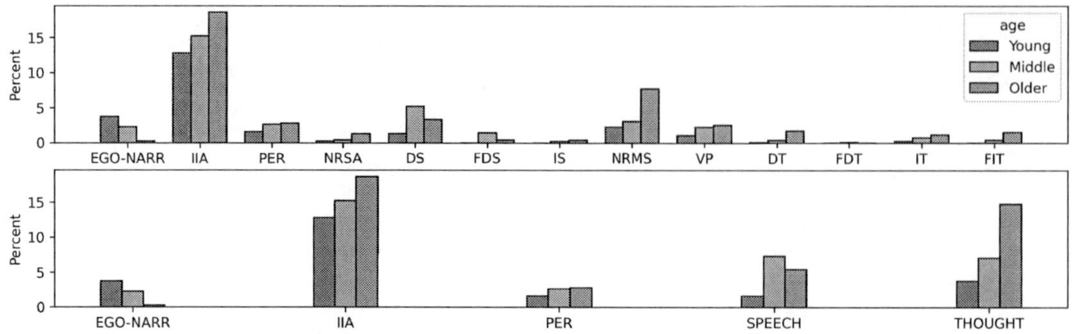

Figure 1: Occurrence of the original and merged CPR types in stories by children in three age groups, in percentages.

type	O_{young}	O_{middle}	O_{old}	E	χ^2	p
EGO-NARR	28	17	2	15.67	21.74	.000*
IIA	96	114	140	116.67	8.39	.015
PER	12	20	21	17.67	2.75	.252
SPEECH	12	55	41	36	26.72	.000*
THOUGHT	28	53	111	64	56.66	.000*

Table 2: Observed frequencies, expected values, and χ^2 statistics with $df = 2$ for all merged CPR types. Since we run 5 separate χ^2 tests on the same variable, α was set to $.05/5 = .01$. * indicates $p < \alpha$.

representation. Dealing with character thought, in turn, is argued to be more advanced on a cognitive level than handling speech, for exactly the reason discussed in the preceding paragraph: thought representation requires the narrator to intrude into character minds, whereas speech representation does not. Following this analysis, plus our own analysis of *ego-narration* in 2.4, the order in which we present the fourteen types in Table 1 can be seen as indicating different stages, ranging from preliminary (*EGO-NARR*), to basic (*IIA, PER*), to intermediate (*NRSA, (F)DS, (F)IS*), to advanced (*NRMS, VP, (F)DT, (F)IT*).

4 Hypothesis Testing and Discussion

4.1 Development: Three Age Groups

For statistical analyses of the observed counts we merged CPR types that are theoretically closely related. In line with the stages discussed above, *NRSA*, *DS*, *FDS*, *IS*, and *FIS* were grouped as *SPEECH*, and *NRMS*, *VP*, *DT*, *FDT*, *IT*, and *FIT* as *THOUGHT*. Character-perspective representation as found in our sample is plotted for both the five merged and fourteen original types in Figure 1. We conducted several χ^2 (chi-square) goodness-of-fit tests to probe whether observed frequencies for a given CPR type differed significantly from a uniform distribution among the three age groups. Test statistics and p-values are given in Table 2, with $\chi^2 = \sum_{k=1}^{n} \frac{(O_k - E_k)^2}{E_k}$, $df = k - 1$.

We see that younger children use a lot more *EGO-NARR*, but older children a lot less compared to the expected value E; the distribution is significantly different from uniform. This suggests children 'outgrow' ego narration, which we argued is a preliminary stage of CPR, and as hypothesised it seems to disappear from children's storytelling as they get older. For both *IIA* and *PER*, which we called basic types of CPR, the distributions do not differ significantly from uniform. Thus, there are no age-specific preferences among children for either *IIA* or *PER*, contra our hypothesis that these basic types occur mainly at young age.

With regard to *SPEECH*, the distribution among age groups is significantly different from uniform. We see little use among young children compared to the expected value E, but a peak in use at middle age and then a slight decrease in use for the older group. This supports our hypothesis that *SPEECH*, which we argued is an intermediate type of CPR, is increasingly used at a later age.

THOUGHT is significantly different from uniformly distributed and seems to take off rather late. The younger and middle groups use less *THOUGHT* compared to the expected value E, whereas the older group uses it a lot more. This pattern observed regarding *THOUGHT* offers clearest support for our prediction that advanced types

	Lexical Complexity				Syntactic Complexity		
Age	$\bar{x}$	s	n	Age	$\bar{x}$	s	n
Young	5.72	.63	176	Young	2.69	.85	176
Middle	5.96	.65	259	Middle	2.70	.97	259
Older	5.99	.63	315	Older	2.75	.85	315

Table 3: Descriptive statistics for lexical complexity (given in utterance perplexity) and syntactic complexity (given in maximum tree depth), for a total of 750 utterances featuring CPR from 150 stories, 50 stories per age group.

	Lexical Complexity		Syntactic Complexity	
Fixed effects	β	SE	β	SE
(Intercept)	5.759*	0.138	2.363*	.182
IIA	.211	.151	.327	.204
PER	-.028	.228	.733*	.318
SPEECH	.331	.238	.002	.329
THOUGHT	.344	.186	.419	.255
Middle	.055	.239	-.051	.306
Older	1.114*	.470	.602	.673
Interactions	β	SE	β	SE
IIA * Middle	.091	.254	.198	.331
PER * Middle	.216	.328	-.201	.448
SPEECH * Middle	.172	.323	.248	.431
THOUGHT * Middle	0.049	.285	-.014	.377
IIA * Older	-.896	.474	-.433	.682
PER * Older	-.575	.521	-.689	.748
SPEECH * Older	-1.022*	.515	-.313	.739
THOUGHT * Older	-1.136*	.488	-.770	.700
Random effects	s	-	s	-
Child (Intercept)	.321	-	.276	-
Residual	.573	-	.862	-

Table 4: Coefficients for two linear mixed models. In both models, only by-child varying intercepts were estimated. The omitted CPR type (*EGO-NARR*) and age group (Young) are the reference categories (i.e., the intercept is the average perplexity/treedepth for an utterance of a young child employing the *ego-narrator* type). * indicates $p < .05$.

of CPR are increasingly applied at a later age.

In summary, children of all ages in our sample tell stories in which character perspectives are represented. As children grow older, perspectives of their characters tend to be fleshed out in more diverse and advanced ways. For the middle group we observe that characters more often speak and have various kinds of thoughts and other mental states. The older group relies even more often on forms of though representation, and slightly less on character speech; possibly using the first partly instead of the latter.

4.2 Linguistic contexts: Lexical and Syntactic Complexity

Next we examine whether more complex types of CPR co-occur with utterances that are lexically and syntactically more complex. We automatically extracted lexical complexity (LC) and syntactic complexity (SC) for each utterance. For LC, we first lemmatised utterances with the spaCy parser (Honnibal and Montani, 2017), and calculated the lexical perplexity; for SC, we also used the spaCy parser to extract the maximum depth of the parsed tree, as described in 2.5. Means and standard deviations of the thus constructed variables are given in Table 3. As can be seen, average differences for both lexical and syntactic complexity are small across the three age groups. Next we employed LC and SC as dependent variables in two linear mixed models. We included our five merged types of CPR as categorical predictors and included interactions with our three age groups, to find out whether different CPR types have significantly different mean LC and SC values, while taking potential age differences into account. Coefficients are given in Table 4. Our overall finding is that the link between lexical and syntactic complexity, and specific types of CPR is not as we anticipated.

We first discuss the results for LC. Here we see that the only significant main effect is Older, which means that with respect to the young *EGO-NARR* reference class, older children use ego narration in utterances that are lexically more complex than young children do. Further, we see two significant negative interactions with *SPEECH* and

THOUGHT, indicating that as we ascend from our reference class to older children that use these intermediate and advanced forms of CPR, the lexical complexity of the utterances decreases, which is contrary to what we hypothesised with respect to LC. We do not see evidence for our hypothesis that average LC for more complex types of CPR is higher compared to ego narration, while taking age differences into account.

Next we elaborate on our results for SC. Here we see no evidence for our hypothesis that more complex forms of CPR co-occur in utterances that have higher average syntactic complexity, while taking age differences into account. Main and interaction effects are all insignificant, except *PER* as main effect, which implies that with respect to our young *EGO-NARR* reference class, the average SC is higher when young children employ *PER* as type of CPR. This is contrary to what we hypothesised in Section 2.6, as this a basic CPR type which we expected to co-occur with less complex syntax.

It appears that our results are not in line with earlier work suggesting that children's more advanced lexical and syntactical skills co-occur with better socio-cognitive skills (as reviewed in e.g. Milligan et al., 2007). One possibility is that the way we looked at lexical and syntactic information in utterances here, provides a too limited view on the contexts in which different types of CPR occur. Given that our previous work demonstrates that lexical richness on the level of the entire stories children tell predicts the occurrence of more sophisticated story characters (van Dijk and van Duijn, 2021), we suggest that automatically extracted information on the story level (as opposed to the utterance level only) could be more helpful for modelling CPR occurrence in the future.

5 Reflection and Conclusion

Our inventory shows that CPR is ubiquitous in freely told children's stories and that it takes many different forms. We discussed that classification of perspective phenomena into a system of CPR types requires knowledge of linguistic and narratological theory, and that it is regularly dependent on thorough analysis of an utterance's context within a story. Reliance on a single annotator is a weakness of this study; however, we believe to have satisfied our goal of building a meaningful (foundation of a) bridge between long-standing research traditions in the Humanities and current approaches in the computational sciences.

Regarding *ego narration* we have identified cases exhibiting a problematic mixing between children's own perspective and the narrator's or characters' perspectives in the story, and argued for seeing these as a preliminary stage of CPR. Also, building on existing work from developmental psychology and cognitive linguistics, we have introduced the types *IIA*, *PER*, and *VP* in our analysis, covering perspectives implied in actions, perceptions, and single lexical units such as 'secretly'. This was particularly useful for getting a grasp on the more basic stages of perspective coordination as present in our sample of children's stories. Although we did not see occurrence of these basic stages peak at younger ages, as we expected, we presented evidence that indeed more complex types are implemented more frequently at later ages.

Furthermore, our aim was to link automatically extracted linguistic information to the occurrence of different types of CPR, while also taking age differences into account. The picture that emerged for lexical and syntactic complexity was more complicated than we anticipated. By taking into account dependency of utterances coming from the same speaker by using random intercepts, and by including interactions with age in our statistical models, we tried to describe as much variation as possible in the language children use when rendering character perspectives. As we saw, overall average differences in lexical and syntactic complexity between ages were small at the outset, and we were not able to link higher linguistic complexity to advanced types of CPR. Here the overall sparse occurrence of several of the individual types likely calls for exploiting a larger part of our story database in the future. We also learned that using perplexity and tree depth to describe the immediate (utterance-level) contexts in which CPR patterns occur, is challenging, suggesting that additional types of linguistic information from wider (story-level) contexts could be needed.

All in all, these findings and lessons encourage us to pursue the line of inquiry set out in this paper. This will also require refining our framework, models, and automatically extracted information in interaction with linguistic and narratological theory, for which additional interdisciplinary cooperation is indispensable.

References

Ian Apperly. 2010. *Mindreaders: the Cognitive Basis of 'Theory of Mind'*. Taylor & Francis.

Ann Banfield. 1973. Narrative style and the grammar of direct and indirect speech. *Foundations of language*, 10(1):1–39.

Kathy. Charmaz. 2006. *Constructing Grounded Theory: A Practical Guide through Qualitative Analysis*. Sage Publications.

Teresa Cremin, Rosie Flewitt, Ben Mardell, and Joan Swann, editors. 2017. *Storytelling in Early Childhood. Enriching language, literacy and classroom culture*. Routledge Abingdon.

Barbara Dancygier. 2011. *The language of stories: A cognitive approach*. Cambridge University Press.

Barbara Dancygier, Weilun Lu, and Arie Verhagen, editors. 2016. *Viewpoint and the Fabric of Meaning: Form and Use of Viewpoint Tools across Languages and Modalities*. De Gruyter Mouton.

Felice Dell'Orletta, Simonetta Montemagni, and Giulia Venturi. 2011. READ–IT: Assessing Readability of Italian Texts with a View to Text Simplification. In *Proceedings of the Second Workshop on Speech and Language Processing for Assistive Technologies*, pages 73–83.

Monika Fludernik. 1996. *Towards a 'natural' narratology*. Routledge.

Shaun Gallagher and Daniel D. Hutto. 2008. Understanding Others Through Primary Interaction and Narrative Practice. In J. Zlatev, T. Racine, C. Sinha, and E. Itkonen, editors, *The Shared Mind: Perspectives on Intersubjectivity.*, pages 17–38. John Benjamins.

Matthew Honnibal and Ines Montani. 2017. SpaCy 2: Natural Language Understanding with Bloom Embeddings, Convolutional Neural Networks and Incremental Parsing.

Ganesh Jawahar, Benoît Sagot, and Djamé Seddah. 2019. What Does BERT Learn about the Structure of Language? In *Proceedings of the 57th Annual Meeting of the Association for Computational Linguistics*, pages 3651–3657.

Franziska Köder. 2016. *Between direct and indirect speech: The acquisition of pronouns in reported speech*. Ph.D. thesis, University of Groningen.

Geoffrey N. Leech and Mick Short. 2007. *Style in fiction: A linguistic introduction to English fictional prose*. Pearson Education.

Uri Margolin. 2014. Narrator. In Peter Hühn et al., editor, *The Living Handbook of Narratology*. Hamburg University.

Bruce McConachie and F Elizabeth Hart. 2006. *Performance and Cognition. Theatre Studies and the Cognitive Turn*. Routledge.

Anne McKeough and Randy Genereux. 2003. Transformation in narrative thought during adolescence: The structure and content of story compositions. *Journal of Educational Psychology*, 95(3):537.

Karen Milligan, Janet Wilde Astington, and Lisa Ain Dack. 2007. Language and theory of mind: Meta-analysis of the relation between language ability and false-belief understanding. *Child development*, 78(2):622–646.

Ageliki Nicolopoulou. 2018. *Pretend and Social Pretend Play: Complexities, Continuities, and Controversies of a Research Field*, Cambridge Handbooks in Psychology, page 183–199. Cambridge University Press.

Ageliki Nicolopoulou and Elizabeth S. Richner. 2007. From Actors to Agents to Persons: The Development of Character Representation in Young Children's Narratives. *Child development*, 78(2):412–429.

José Sanders. 2010. Intertwined voices: Journalists' modes of representing source information in journalistic subgenres. *English Text Construction*, 3(2):226–249.

Frenette Southwood and Ann F. Russell. 2004. Comparison of Conversation, Freeplay, and Story Generation as Methods of Language Sample Elicitation. *Journal of Speech, Language and Hearing Research*, 47(2):366–376.

Brian Sutton-Smith. 1986. Children's fiction making. In T.R. Sarbin, editor, *Narrative psychology: The storied nature of human conduct*, pages 67–90. Praeger Publishers/Greenwood Publishing Group.

Agnes Tellings, Nelleke Oostdijk, Iris Monster, Franc Grootjen, and Antal Van Den Bosch. 2018. BasiScript: A corpus of contemporary Dutch texts written by primary school children. *International Journal of Corpus Linguistics*, 23(4):494–508.

Bram M.A. van Dijk and Max J. van Duijn. 2021. Modelling Characters' Mental Depth in Stories Told by Children Aged 4-10. In *Proceedings of the annual meeting of the cognitive science society*, pages 2384–2391. The Cognitive Science Society.

Max van Duijn and Arie Verhagen. 2018. Beyond triadic communication: A three-dimensional conceptual space for modelling intersubjectivity. *Pragmatics & Cognition*, 25(2):384–416.

Linde van Schuppen, Kobie. van Krieken, and José Sanders. 2020. Variations in Viewpoint Presentation: The 'Pear Story' as Told by People with a Schizophrenia Diagnosis. *Open Library of Humanities*, 6(2):2.

Lieven Vandelanotte. 2009. Speech and thought representation in english. In *Speech and Thought Representation in English*. De Gruyter Mouton.

Anne Vermeer. 2001. Breadth and depth of vocabulary in relation to L1/L2 acquisition and frequency of input. *Applied psycholinguistics*, 22(2):217–234.

Blakey Vermeule. 2009. *Why Do We Care About Literary Characters?* John Hopkins University Press.

Peter Verstraten. 2009. *Film Narratology*. University of Toronto Press.

Sonja Zeman. 2020. Parameters of narrative perspectivization: The narrator. *Open Library of Humanities*, 6(2):28.

Lisa Zunshine. 2019. What Mary Poppins Knew: Theory of Mind, Children's Literature, History. *Narrative*, 27:1–29.

Author Index

Association for Computational Linguistics
209 N. Eighth Street
Stroudsburg, Pennsylvania 18360

ISBN 978-1-7138-5645-0

CURRAN ASSOCIATES INC.
proceedings.com